Navigating Policy and Practice in the Great Recession

Navigating Policy and Practice in the Great Recession

STACEY BORASKY

MIGUEL FERGUSON

OXFORD

UNIVERSITY PRESS

OXFORD
UNIVERSITY PRESS

Oxford University Press is a department of the University of Oxford. It furthers
the University's objective of excellence in research, scholarship, and education
by publishing worldwide. Oxford is a registered trade mark of Oxford University
Press in the UK and certain other countries.

Published in the United States of America by Oxford University Press
198 Madison Avenue, New York, NY 10016, United States of America.

Library of Congress Cataloging-in-Publication Data
Names: Borasky, Stacey, author. | Ferguson, Miguel, author.
Title: Navigating policy and practice in the Great Recession /
Stacey Borasky, Miguel Ferguson.
Description: New York, NY : Oxford University Press, [2018] |
Includes bibliographical references and index.
Identifiers: LCCN 2017052922 (print) | LCCN 2018010978 (ebook) |
ISBN 9780190871093 (updf) | ISBN 9780190871109 (epub) |
ISBN 9780190871086 (pbk. : alk. paper)
Subjects: LCSH: Social service—United States. |
Social work administration—United States. | Public welfare—United States. |
Recessions—Social aspects—United States.
Classification: LCC HV91 (ebook) | LCC HV91.B597 2018 (print) |
DDC 361.6/10973—dc23
LC record available at https://lccn.loc.gov/2017052922

1 3 5 7 9 8 6 4 2

Printed by Webcom, Inc., Canada

Navigating Policy and Practice in the Great Recession

STACEY BORASKY
MIGUEL FERGUSON

OXFORD
UNIVERSITY PRESS

OXFORD
UNIVERSITY PRESS

Oxford University Press is a department of the University of Oxford. It furthers
the University's objective of excellence in research, scholarship, and education
by publishing worldwide. Oxford is a registered trade mark of Oxford University
Press in the UK and certain other countries.

Published in the United States of America by Oxford University Press
198 Madison Avenue, New York, NY 10016, United States of America.

© Oxford University Press 2018

Library of Congress Cataloging-in-Publication Data
Names: Borasky, Stacey, author. | Ferguson, Miguel, author.
Title: Navigating policy and practice in the Great Recession /
Stacey Borasky, Miguel Ferguson.
Description: New York, NY : Oxford University Press, [2018] |
Includes bibliographical references and index.
Identifiers: LCCN 2017052922 (print) | LCCN 2018010978 (ebook) |
ISBN 9780190871093 (updf) | ISBN 9780190871109 (epub) |
ISBN 9780190871086 (pbk. : alk. paper)
Subjects: LCSH: Social service—United States. |
Social work administration—United States. | Public welfare—United States. |
Recessions—Social aspects—United States.
Classification: LCC HV91 (ebook) | LCC HV91.B597 2018 (print) |
DDC 361.6/10973—dc23
LC record available at https://lccn.loc.gov/2017052922

1 3 5 7 9 8 6 4 2

Printed by Webcom, Inc., Canada

Contents

Foreword

SOCIAL WORKERS WHO lead agencies must balance the needs of clients with all the responsibilities of their position. The challenges faced include acquiring resources to serve clients, being fair employers for staff, handling issues related to the board of directors, responding to community economic need, and creating for themselves a sustainable work-life balance, among other things.

The realities of such challenges are not easily communicated in typical textbooks. That is why *Navigating Policy and Practice in the Great Recession* is different (and much needed). This book is a sequel to *Caught in the Storm: Navigating Policy and Practice in the Welfare Reform Era* (2010). In this book, readers return to the story of Helping Hands, a non-profit agency set in the fictional town of River City. Covering a period of seven years during and immediately after the Great Recession, the story is told from the viewpoint of Martha White, the dedicated executive director who tirelessly strives to keep the agency open and serve a growing number of destitute clients. Martha is assisted by an able staff of full-time employees and interns and others we meet as the book progresses.

The narrative begins in September 2007. The board of directors is convening, and three new members are attending their first meeting. A successful program evaluation report is on the agenda, as are topics such as government funding for faith-based organizations and the board's upcoming evaluation of Martha. On the way home, Martha gets her first glimpse into the housing crisis of that time, when neighbors fall months behind on their home payments and are forced to move. All of this is in the first chapter, and the story is off and running.

Chapter 2 contains information about an embezzling CEO of another agency, the results of Martha's evaluation, and the threat of a successful program being "defunded" by the state, despite positive results. It ends with

Martha being appointed by the mayor of River City to chair a Commission of Inquiry regarding the embezzlement.

Later chapters continue in this style, leading readers through a dizzying array of situations that happen in the non-profit sector. By the end of the book in the summer of 2014, readers will have learned important lessons about human service activities and leadership, board members' responsibilities, the impact of politics and policy on agencies, the never-ending search for sufficient appropriate funding, community organizing, and a host of other topics. The precipitating factors of the Great Recession, the Troubled Asset Relief Program (TARP), the election of President Obama, the American Recovery and Reinvestment (ARRA) and Affordable Care Acts, housing discrimination and foreclosure, marriage equality, and the Occupy movements are introduced and discussed as they impact the staff and clients of Helping Hands and residents of River City. These are a tumultuous seven years, but, organized from Martha's vantage, readers will see macro-practice in action and come to understand how the personal and political are a seamless fabric.

As you traverse this engaging story, you will have the benefit of beautiful artwork by veteran graphic artist Sharon Rudahl, who skillfully highlights scenes from the book. The graphic art, dialogue, and vivid vignettes of agency life provide a sense of how the "real world" operates and will take readers down unexpected paths. If you think that policy is boring or only for wonks, this book (and *Caught in the Storm* before it) will change your mind. Additional resources are listed after every chapter so readers can explore, from a more academic perspective, the topics covered and the questions raised.

Readers are with Martha and her staff, overhearing their conversations, eavesdropping on their disagreements, and learning with them as they face the results of their decisions. After encountering Martha and Helping Hands, you and your fellow readers will share stories—as workers in human service agencies, clients of organizations, or perhaps as people who have lived through or participated in the historic events that marked the years of the Great Recession.

The final few pages describe an unexpected offer given to Martha to leave her job as director of Helping Hands. We do not know what her decision is as we close the cover. Will this open the door to another book? Only time will tell. In any case, take the time to enjoy this nontraditional text. It is packed with learning opportunities and readers will emerge with a better understanding of what it means to be a social worker.

Richard Hoefer, PhD
University of Texas at Arlington

Acknowledgments

AFTER MORE THAN twenty years in social work education, there are many people to whom I owe debts of gratitude. My students over the years often inspired me to experiment in my teaching methods and take risks. This book is another one of those risks, as it is unique for a textbook in many ways. Just as I was rewarded by my students for stretching their minds and outlooks and creating interesting challenges for them academically, this book offers its own reward in pushing social work education to be creative.

I am also grateful to both my former clients and my colleagues in social work practice. My experiences in child welfare, mental health, and community organizing shaped Martha's perspective in this book. We must always remember that the people with whom we work teach us every day, and social workers must allow that learning to shape their responses to clients and to policies that affect their lives.

Finally, I owe a debt of gratitude to my family, from my husband to my children and parents, for their years of support for my career. My ability to write this book is only possible due to their constant love and always having my back. I love you all.

SB

TO MY WIFE, who saved me.

MF

List of Characters

Martha	Executive Director of Helping Hands
Julia	Martha's administrative assistant
Ruth	Social Services Coordinator at Helping Hands and former NYC teacher born in the Dominican Republic
Melissa	Former social work intern and current caseworker at Helping Hands
Rev. Anderson	Pastor whose church partnered with Helping Hands
Robert Martínez	New member of Helping Hands advisory board
Florence Bossier	New member of Helping Hands advisory board
Deena Perkins	Former client and new member of Helping Hands advisory board
Carlene Francis	Business owner and chair of Helping Hands advisory board
Dr. Alvin Gault	Professor and member of Helping Hands advisory board
Dr. Annabelle Barr	Professor, Helping Hands program evaluator
Alice Chan	Executive Director of non-profit, colleague of Martha
Mr./Mrs. Johnson	Elderly neighbors of Martha
Brandon and Jessie	Martha's twin son and daughter
Allen	Martha's husband

Abbreviations

ACA	Affordable Care Act
ACF	Administration for Children and Families
ARRA	American Recovery and Reinvestment Act of 2009
CAA	Community Action Agency
CASA	Court Appointed Special Advocate
CCS	Council of Community Services
CDO	Collateralized Debt Obligation
CNA	Certified Nursing Assistants
CPS	Child Protective Services
DCS	Department of Children's Services
DHS	Department of Human Services
Dodd-Frank	Wall Street Reform and Consumer Protection Act
EITC	Earned Income Tax Credit
MIECHV	Maternal Infant, and Early Childhood Home Visiting Program
RFP	Request for Proposals
SNAP	Supplemental Nutrition Assistance Program
TARP	Troubled Asset Relief Program
WIC	Women, Infants, and Children (Special Supplemental Nutrition Program)

Navigating Policy and Practice in the Great Recession

I

A New Beginning

September 2007

On a warm Monday morning, Martha leaned back in her office chair and closed her eyes. She couldn't believe how quickly time had passed. Recently she and her husband Allen had participated in parent orientation weekends at two separate universities. Martha had accompanied her daughter Jessie to an out-of-state university, while Allen had accompanied Brandon, Jessie's twin brother, to Martha's alma mater, the state university located in River City. She didn't know what was more shocking, returning to a home without the twins or being confronted with the costs of supporting two kids in college. Luckily, she and Allen had the benefit of Tomorrow Funds that her parents had purchased when the twins were born. A state-administered program, Tomorrow Funds allowed the purchase of tuition credits that could be applied in the future. Over the years she and Allen had added money to the fund for the kids, but the sacrifice appeared to be well worth it. Tuition at universities everywhere had gone up many times the rate of inflation since Martha had attended school in the 1980s. She remembered receiving a full-ride scholarship as an undergrad that also covered books and fees—for $1,000 a year. Tuition for her last semester of grad school in social work had been $500. Now tuition was almost $5,000 a semester and much higher for out-of-state students. Though many states had cancelled versions of college tuition investment programs after the dot com bust in the early 2000s, Martha's state had thankfully continued to implement it.

Martha opened her eyes to find her administrative assistant Julia standing at her door. Martha had hired Julia a few years back when she was recently divorced and struggling to raise two boys, mostly on her own. Julia had proven to be energetic and organized—and someone who had definite opinions about what the clients they served should do to improve their situations.

"Did someone get in late last night?" Julia asked.

"Yes," said Martha, "I got the last flight out because I knew it was going to take time to set Jessie up in her dorm. Four girls in one room, I'm glad I don't have to be a part of that," Martha joked.

"And what about Brandon?" Julia asked. "For some reason I don't see Allen trudging around a store looking for bedspreads and kitchen utensils."

"As usual, he got off easy," Martha laughed. "Brandon's sharing a furnished garage apartment with one of his high school buddies near campus."

"If he keeps it like my boys keep their room, I swear you'll need a Hazmat suit when you visit, mark my words," Julia said, shaking her head.

"I hope he'll be too busy to make much of a mess," Martha replied. "He's taking 15 credits, working part-time, and still insists he wants to try and walk-on to the basketball team. And he's signed up for a course with Dr. Gault called 'Poverty in America in Non-Fiction and Film.'" Dr. Gault, a social work professor Martha first met while pursuing her master's of social work, had been one of the first board members Martha had recruited when she became executive director of Helping Hands, a small non-profit social service organization.

"Sounds like he's getting off to a running start," said Julia, "and speaking of which . . ." She held out a large manila envelope.

"Are those the copies of the evaluation report?" Martha asked.

"Yep," Julia responded, placing them in front of Martha on her cluttered desk. "One for each board member. Are they all coming today?"

"As far as I know," Martha said as she opened the envelope. The evaluation report Martha planned to discuss at the board meeting had just been completed by Dr. Annabelle Barr, a colleague of Dr. Gault in the School of Social Work. Dr. Barr's report was nothing short of glowing, and Martha was excited to share the findings with her board.

A few minutes before noon, Martha and Julia arrived at Casa Maya, the restaurant owned by former board member Carlos Hernandez. With his typical generosity, Carlos had invited Martha and the board members to conduct their meeting in a private room at his restaurant. It was an important meeting. In addition to sharing information on the evaluation report and the agency's other functions, Martha was introducing three new members to the rest of the board. As usual, Carlos was in the foyer, greeting customers as they arrived for lunch.

BOARD MEETING OF HELPING HANDS AT CARLOS' RESTAURANT

SHARON RUDAHL 2014

"Marta and Julia, bienvenidos!" he exclaimed while giving them both a hug. Though he spoke impeccable English, Carlos always delighted in pronouncing names in his own way and sprinkling Spanish throughout his conversations.

"You are the only one who calls me 'hoo-lee-uh,' Carlos, but I really like it," replied Julia with a smile as she returned his hug.

"I've already met the new board members," said Carlos as he led them to a room in the back of the restaurant. "They seem like they are ready to go!"

Martha and Julia entered to see that Robert Martinez, Florence Bossier, and Deena Perkins were already chatting.

"I just told Robert that he is even better looking in person than he is on TV!" Florence joked to Martha as she greeted her new board members. Robert laughed but was clearly embarrassed. His family ran two successful car dealerships in River City, and Robert could often be seen on commercials that ran on local stations. Though he was young, Martha was aware that he was a savvy businessman and had pushed his family to work with customers who had less than stellar credit histories. Florence, a retired state worker, had been recommended to the Helping Hands board by Rev. Anderson, who had worked with Martha on a welfare-to-work grant for the last three years. Rev. Anderson described her to Martha as a "force of nature" in her work as a court-appointed special advocate (CASA) volunteer. She was also an active member of the National Association for the Advancement of Colored People and had recently focused her efforts on housing discrimination against African Americans in River City. Deena was a former client of Helping Hands who had successfully participated in a Certified Nursing Training welfare-to-work program that Helping Hands had administered a couple of years earlier. She felt serving on the board was not only a way of giving back to the agency that had been so instrumental in her success but also allowed her to bring a client's perspective to decisions regarding services, staffing, and other issues that directly impacted the clients that Helping Hands served.

After the other board members arrived, it was time for introductions. In addition to the new members, Martha was happy to introduce Carlene Francis, who replaced Carlos as chair of the board, and Dr. Gault. Martha provided a brief recap of Helping Hands activities for the benefit of the new board members. "Helping Hands began as a community action agency in the 1960s, and over the last four decades we have continued our mission to serve low-income populations in River City and beyond." Glancing at Robert and taking note of his relative youth, Martha thought it would be wise to provide a brief description of community action agencies.

"Community action agencies were formed during the War on Poverty, and even though many think that the War on Poverty is a vestige from a bygone era, community action agencies have continued to operate all over the country." Martha held up a report for the board members to see, titled *Rooting Out Poverty: A Campaign by America's Community Action Network.* "I just received this, and I'm going to pass it around. There are over a thousand community action agencies, and this is the theme that agencies around the country are going to follow." She handed the report to Carlene. "For the last three years, we have been involved with community partners in providing services to Katrina evacuees and work preparation support as part of a welfare-to-work program funded by the Department of Human Services. These services mesh well with the campaign to maximize participation, build a better economy, invest in the future, promote equal opportunity, and create healthy people and places."

Carlene interrupted, "Could we each get a copy of this report?" she asked.

"Certainly," said Martha as she glanced at Julia, who nodded affirmatively. "We just didn't want to overwhelm you with information because, as you can all see, each of you has a copy of the latest evaluation report we have received from the DHS evaluator." Practically in unison, the board members picked up their copy of the report and began looking them over. "In a nutshell," Martha continued with a glance to Deena, "three years ago we began to provide welfare-to-work services in a program funded by DHS. The original program provided a three-week prep course and financial support for students seeking to become certified nursing assistants. Though we met program goals, the evaluation of that program found that while many graduates were able to find work as CNAs, the low wages and nontraditional schedules posed a hardship."

"Can I ask a question?" said Robert.

"Of course," replied Martha. "Fire away."

"Well, is the program evaluated on whether or not Helping Hands did what it said it was going to do or on the effects of the program? Because it seems a bit ridiculous to evaluate a program on factors it can't control, like wages and schedules."

"May I?" interjected Dr. Gault, looking at Martha. She gestured her approval. "You ask a great question, Robert, but the answer really has two parts. The evaluation was conducted by one of my colleagues through the Center for Social Service Research. It was both a process evaluation and an outcome evaluation. Like the name implies, a process evaluation looks at the system that the program has set up, marketing, recruitment, staff training, service fidelity, etc. In years past it may have been enough to show that you did what you proposed to do. But more and more legislators want to see a significant bang for the buck, so measuring the outcomes of program implementation has become more important over time."

In response to Dr. Gault's comments, Martha repeated a story she had been told by a DHS caseworker about a state program to encourage low-income households to apply for food stamps, a program that brought in $50 for every dollar spent on outreach, which had recently been cut by the legislature.

"That doesn't make much business sense to me," Robert said. "Spending a dollar to get back fifty is a no-brainer!"

"It's a good example of how the legislature can operate, and why funding for non-profits can be so mercurial," replied Dr. Gault in his typical academic style.

"These are serious issues," said Martha, "but in the interest of time I'd like to keep things moving. A year ago, we put together a revised proposal for another two-year grant with DHS. We decided to work with River City Community College again but this time provide support for students pursuing degrees in different allied health fields. If you turn to the findings section on page 12, you can see that 97% of the graduates from the first year of the program have found work, and the average starting wage is over $15 an hour."

A general murmur of approval went through the room.

"The next page includes quotes from some of the graduates that Dr. Barr interviewed," continued Martha, "and they are really telling. They were specifically asked if they could have gotten through the program without the help we provided, and almost every one of them said no."

"These are excellent findings, Martha," Dr. Gault intoned. "You responded to the critique made of the first program and put together some definite improvements. Let me be the first to commend you and your staff for such a well-developed project."

"It all started with a brainstorming session I had with Carlene one day," Martha replied, inwardly pleased to hear the praise from the professor, who could often be very critical.

Carlene added her own thoughts. "My favorite line in this report is when it refers to our allied health program as a *gold standard* for other programs to follow. We identified an employment niche, worked with the college to recruit eligible students, and then plugged gaps in support. We provided gas vouchers for students who had to travel long distances to attend classes and even paid for testing and licensing exams after they finished their coursework. I wish I could take credit, but that sort of attention to detail has Martha's name all over it."

Martha waved off the compliment with her typical humility. "I think it really underscores what an important role the board plays in Helping Hands. We rely on your expertise and input every step of the way."

Deena spoke up. "I know we discussed the duties when you asked if I would join the board, Martha, but could you please describe them again? This is all new to me."

"I wouldn't mind hearing about them again either," said Florence, looking reassuringly at Deena.

"Absolutely," said Martha. "The board oversees the financial management of Helping Hands and also provides support and supervision for me in my role as executive director. At our monthly meetings you will be given copies of financial documents and any other material that speaks to the health of the agency."

"Such as program evaluations," interjected Dr. Gault, holding up a copy of the welfare-to-work evaluation they had been discussing.

"We also rely on your feedback regarding request for proposals and other funding possibilities that come up," Martha continued.

"Request for proposals?" Robert asked, looking around at the other board members.

"Excuse my non-profit jargon," Martha replied. "Request for proposals are grant opportunities, usually put out by some government office or a philanthropic organization, that seek to fund proposals to implement a social service program."

"So the welfare-to-work program got funded because you answered a request for proposals from DHS?" Robert quickly asked.

"That's exactly what happened," said Martha, pleased that Robert was such a quick study. "And for the first round we only had three weeks to put it together."

"I seem to remember we had an emergency board meeting to discuss that one," said Dr. Gault.

"Yes," said Martha, "it was a significant amount of money, but it asked us to provide services we had never offered before."

"And it was pretty clear that programs that partnered with faith-based organizations would have an edge," added Carlene.

Dr. Gault couldn't help going into professor mode. Speaking to the three new members, he noted that the welfare-to-work programs were part of a push by the Bush administration to emphasize the participation of faith-based organizations in the delivery of social services under the Office of Faith-Based and Community Initiatives.

"In truth," he finished, "he actually started similar programs while he was governor of Texas."

"I didn't know all the background, but I do know that the childcare I received at Rev. Anderson's church allowed me to finish the CNA program at River City," responded Deena, referring to the first welfare-to-work program that Helping Hands had implemented. She and her daughter Jackie had both completed the CNA program, and now each worked separate shifts at a local facility in order to take care of Jackie's kids while the other was at work.

"Let me get this straight," said Robert. "Are we talking faith-based organizations like Catholic Charities and Lutheran Social Services or individual churches?"

"Well, both really," replied Martha. "We worked directly with Rev. Anderson's church because I have known him for a number of years and I knew that his church had a well-established childcare program."

"But the church was being paid with government money?" Robert asked quizzically.

Martha could see where this was going but wanted to make sure she provided the level of detail that Robert's question demanded. "Well, the most accurate explanation would be to say that Rev. Anderson's church paid the childcare workers that were employed as part of the welfare-to-work program, and then DHS reimbursed them for the expenses they incurred."

Somewhat defensively, Florence took the opportunity to jump in the conversation. "I'm a member of Rev. Anderson's congregation, and I've talked with him about this program. The church did not charge for the space and even threw in meals and transportation for the kids."

"I don't think Robert was implying any wrongdoing on the church's part, Florence," said Martha, in an attempt to keep the conversation from becoming overheated.

Robert reached over and touched Florence's hand in a mollifying way. "No, I'm not implying anything underhanded about the church at all. I'm just surprised to hear about the direct government, or perhaps indirect would be the better word, funding of church services."

"I understand where you're coming from, Robert," said Dr. Gault. "But somewhat ironically, President Bush's executive order with regard to the faith-based initiative mandated that government agencies not discriminate *against* churches and faith-based groups in funding social services. There's actually a long history of government support for faith-based charities. Just think of the religiously affiliated hospitals in River City. They obviously get paid by Medicaid and Medicare funds, just like any other hospital. The tipping point, as I understand it, is whether the services themselves are religious in nature."

"I hadn't thought of it like that," said Robert.

"And that was one of the questions we discussed at that first meeting," said Martha, bringing the conversation around full circle. "Issues like this are going to come up, and I really hope that this board will always be able to openly discuss these matters."

As if on cue, Carlos entered the room with plates of food in each hand, followed by two waiters. The aroma of the southern Mexican cuisine filled the room. While they ate, Martha was able to learn more about Florence's work as a CASA volunteer. She was amazed at Florence's willingness, though just a volunteer, to go the extra mile as an advocate for children in the foster care system. She was clearly a bulldog for causes she believed in, and Martha felt confident that Helping Hands would also benefit from her years of experience working in state government.

Before the meeting ended, Carlene let the new board members know that this was the year that the board was supposed to carry out a biannual evaluation of Martha's work as executive director. Martha had been at Helping Hands long enough to experience several evaluations and always looked forward to the feedback she received about the way in which her leadership helped to fulfill the mission of the agency. This year, Carlene had proposed to implement a 360-degree feedback evaluation process when gathering information for Martha's evaluation. Carlene had received training on the use of this model at a conference for small business owners. The 360-degree feedback model, also sometimes referred to as multirater or multisource feedback, uses feedback from a variety of individuals within a person's daily work circle. Peers, staff, clients, and the individual being evaluated complete a performance assessment. In Martha's case, this process was particularly exciting, as she had been a director for many years and wanted to use the process to target growth areas for herself and her professional development. Her biggest fear was that she would become stagnant; she believed in lifelong learning and personal and professional growth, even if one has reached the level of executive director.

Carlene explained to the board and Martha how information would be gathered from the staff and a few selected clients of Helping Hands in order to inform their evaluation. She also described the type of self-assessment Martha would conduct so that her perspective was included. Each group would provide feedback related to the functions they perform or the services they receive and evaluate Martha's role in helping them personally and in conducting the daily operations of the agency.

"I'm really looking forward to this evaluation, and that's not something you usually hear people say," Martha said as she bid everyone farewell.

Driving back to Helping Hands with Martha after the meeting, Julia processed what had taken place. "I didn't get a chance to speak with Florence much, but Robert sure seemed to hit the ground running."

"Yes, he certainly did," said Martha, somewhat circumspectly.

"Do I detect some hesitance?" asked Julia as Martha turned the car into traffic.

"No, not really," said Martha. "It's very clear that he has a sharp eye about things, and I suspect that he will pay very close attention to the financial details of our programs. And after all, he's not the only business owner on the board," she said, referring to Carlene and the floral shop that she owned.

"True enough," said Julia, "but at least Carlene had experience working at Child Protective Services before she became a business owner." Martha nodded in agreement and inwardly wondered about the impact that all of the new members would have on her board.

After work, Martha picked up a burger and some fries for Allen from a locally owned restaurant that had just opened a few months before. She planned to eat the leftovers she had brought from lunch at Casa Maya. As she turned on to her street, she saw an elderly couple walking, a familiar sight in her neighborhood. Mr. and Mrs. Johnson were one of the first residents of the neighborhood and old friends of Martha's parents. Mr. Johnson had lost his eyesight a few years earlier due to macular degeneration and now relied on his wife's arm as they walked slowly down the street. She could see their house down the road, with some of Mrs. Johnson's beautiful azaleas still blooming off her porch.

Turning in to her driveway, Martha was surprised to see a moving truck at the house two doors down. She didn't remember seeing any For Sale sign in the front yard and had enjoyed a brief but pleasant chat with her neighbor at the mailbox just a week or so earlier. Martha searched her memory but could not remember her saying anything about moving. At dinner, she mentioned it to Allen.

"Yeah, I saw the truck too," he said between bites of his burger. Clearly he knew no more about the situation than Martha. "I tell you what though," he said, wiping his mouth with a napkin, "after I finish eating I'll go talk to Doug and see what's up."

"That would be great," said Martha, "because you know him a lot better than I know Nancy."

Allen and Doug saw each other somewhat frequently in neighborhood pick-up basketball games that Allen referred to as the "old guys' half-court league."

"Come to think of it, though, he hasn't showed up to play in a while."

Martha got up from the table and took some pie out of the refrigerator. The kitchen seemed so quiet without the twins, who usually had a friend or two in tow. "I haven't told you about my board meeting," Martha said as Allen

A MOVING VAN at MARTHA'S NEIGHBORS HOUSE~

hastened to add a scoop of ice cream to the pie. She described her impressions of the meeting and highlighted how the new members brought different skill sets and experiences than her previous board members. "Robert has no social service experience, but I asked him to join because he has a reputation for being willing to work with low-income folks and people with questionable credit histories."

"Well, ultimately, he's making money on the deals, right?" Allen interjected.

"I suppose," said Martha as she sat back down at the table. "I like that he gives people a second chance. I mean, there probably is an element of risk." Allen shrugged his shoulders in a somewhat disinterested fashion, but Martha continued. "Funny thing is, Julia was really suspicious of him due to some of his questions about our funding."

"He wouldn't be the first person she was suspicious of," Allen quickly retorted.

Martha chuckled at his spot-on assessment of Julia. "I'm hopeful he and this group will be a real asset to me."

"Well," Allen replied while taking his empty plate to the sink, "I hope you get lots of help so it doesn't all fall on your shoulders."

Martha knew there was much behind his comment. She and Allen had often discussed her hectic work life and the heavy demands that her executive director duties placed on her and, by extension, the family. But before she could respond, Allen was already walking out the door.

Discussion Questions

1. What are the basic programs offered by community action agencies across the country? What has changed for these agencies since their introduction during the War on Poverty in the 1960s?

2. If you were Martha, what types of people would you ask to serve on the board of directors of Helping Hands? What skills or knowledge bases would you seek in these individuals? Discuss the reasons for your answers.

3. Martha presents the first comprehensive evaluation of Helping Hands' welfare reform program to the board in this chapter. If you were a board member, what questions would you hope to see on a program evaluation? What data is most important for the agency? How would you use the data for future planning?

4. Discuss the pros and cons of operating budgets based predominantly on grant funding and donations. What are other forms of funding agencies might have for services in addition to these options? If you were an agency director, what types of funding would you seek and why?

Potential Assignments

1. Have students research the initial community action agencies structure and services as compared to current programming. Incorporate political

changes at the federal, state, and local levels that affected the operations of these agencies.

2. Ask students to create a fictional agency and create the management structure and composition from the board of directors to agency supervisory positions. Have them explain the agency's mission and goals, clients to be served, and services offered. They should then justify the structure and composition of the board and supervisors on the basis of education, experiences, skills, and community connections in relation to services and clients served.

3. Have students design a program evaluation for a non-profit agency–based program of your choice. They should create methods for process evaluation and outcome evaluations. If you use a field placement agency and program, students may work with staff there to develop these tools for their use.

4. Using the US Department of Health and Human Services website, assign students to different agencies to research federal funding opportunities through the RFP process. Their research should include a review of each component of the RFP and pay particular attention to the scoring process for proposals. For example, on a scale of 100, grants are typically broken down into separate sections, with each section worth points toward the total 100 possible. They should discuss why more weight is given to one section over another (i.e., what is most important). Have students present their selected RFP to the class, and ask that they discuss the weights given to each section of the grant proposal. Also ask that they describe the funding amounts available, time frame (e.g., three years, five years, etc.), and if matching funds are required.

Suggested Readings

Building an effective advisory committee. (n.d.). Mentoring Resource Center Fact Sheet, US Department of Education. Retrieved from http://educationnorthwest. org/sites/default/files/factsheet21.pdf

DeNisi, A. S., & Kluger, A. N. (2000). Feedback effectiveness: Can 360-degree appraisals be improved? *The Academy of Management Executive, 14*(1), 129–139.

Golden, Olivia. (2012, September 25). Welfare waivers gives states a choice. Retrieved from http://www.urban.org/research/publication/welfare-waivers-give-states-choice

Greenstein, Robert. (2016, July 6). Welfare reform and the safety net: Evidence contradicts likely assumptions behind forthcoming GOP poverty plan. Center on Budget and Policy Priorities. Retrieved from http://www.cbpp.org/research/ family-income-support/welfare-reform-and-the-safety-net

Olivas, Michael A. (2003). State college savings and prepaid tuition plans: A reappraisal and review. *Journal of Law & Education, 32*, 475–514.

Rooting out poverty: A campaign by America's Community Action Network. (n.d.). Retrieved from http://compa.nonprofitsoapbox.com/storage/cap/documents/rop.pdf

Weisz, V., & Thai, N. (2003). The court-appointed special advocate (CASA) program: Bringing information to child abuse & neglect cases. *Child Maltreatment, 8*(3), 204–210.

2

Facing the Future

September 2007

Martha woke the next morning after a fitful night's sleep. Allen had spoken to the neighbors after dinner and found out their house was being foreclosed. Doug had sheepishly admitted that he had been out of work for five months. They had been drawing on their modest savings but could not afford to pay the mortgage for the past few months. Doug said their plan was to move in with his wife's parents in another state. As Martha thought about the situation it occurred to her that an unusually high number of houses had gone up for sale in her neighborhood over the past few years, but she had chalked it up to owners taking advantage of the super-heated real estate market. She now wondered how many of those homeowners had been forced to sell due to a spell of unemployment or because mortgage payments had become too high. Regardless, the neighborhood seemed to have taken on a different feel since she and Allen had moved in after the birth of the twins. Long-term owners like the Johnsons were fewer and fewer in number, and most of the new residents were busy professionals who mostly kept to themselves.

Martha retrieved the paper from her driveway and sat down to enjoy a cup of coffee. With the twins now gone, her morning ritual had become quiet and relaxing, with none of the frenetic commotion that came with seeing the two of them off to school. The chance to grab a few minutes of peace had turned Martha into an early-morning riser, but now the silence did not offer the respite that she had once prized. Today, the headlines caught her attention. One discussed the ongoing protests over the "Jena 6" and the severe criminal justice treatment that six African American youth in Jena, Louisiana, had received for what appeared to be a schoolyard fight. Another discussed President Bush's threat to veto a bill that sought to expand health care for uninsured children.

But it was the headline on the bottom of the page that caught her attention. It read: "DIRECTOR OF LOCAL NON-PROFIT MISSING." Helping Hands was part of a consortium of human service agencies in River City called the Council of Community Services (CCS), and Martha was concerned that some wrongdoing had befallen a community colleague. However, by the end of the first paragraph it was clear that this was not a case of abduction but potential financial malfeasance on the part of the director, who had disappeared after the board had demanded an independent audit of the agency's books. Martha had met the director many times at CCS meetings and had always been impressed with her energy and commitment to children. Indeed, the article noted that the director had single-handedly increased the size and scope of the agency's activities over the years, introducing an infant pantry, parent training courses, a sizeable children's library, and caseworkers with expertise in play therapy for children who had experienced abuse and neglect.

Martha recognized the names of some of the board members cited in the article as prominent members of the business community and shook her head when she read that the mayor's wife was also a member of the board. Though the details in the article were sketchy, Martha knew there would be potential fallout within city politics and in the non-profit world. It had often been repeated at CCS meetings that the consortium was only as strong as its weakest link. I'm afraid we're going to see how true that is, she thought to herself as she finished the article.

At work, Martha was at her desk when Julia came in holding the newspaper. "Did you see the paper today?" Julia asked.

"Yes, I did," said Martha, not surprised by Julia's breathless style. "Are you referring to the article about Patty at The Children's Corner?"

"I sure am! What the heck is going on? Are they saying she just kept sloppy books or that she actually took money, or left the country, or what?"

"I don't know any more than you do," Martha replied. "But the article was frustrating because it seemed to bring up more questions than it answered."

Julia's excited questioning attracted the attention of Ruth, the social services coordinator, who made a beeline for Martha's office upon hearing the conversation.

"Que pasó, pues?" she asked, looking first at Julia and then Martha. Ruth was a former New York City schoolteacher who had emigrated to the United States from the Dominican Republic after the US military invasion in the 1960s. Like Carlos, she also liked to sprinkle Spanish into conversations.

Julia showed her the paper. "This article talks about how the director of The Children's Corner, Patty—."

"Ortiz," Ruth said before Julia could look up the name in the article.

"You know her?" asked Martha, interested now in the connection that had just emerged.

"Not well," said Ruth. "Her husband is Dominican, and . . . I guess you could say that we've crossed paths a few times at social events."

"Do I detect something that you're not sharing?" asked Julia, picking up on the hesitation in Ruth's response.

"It's just . . ;" said Ruth, searching for the right words. "She and her husband have hosted a couple of events at their house, and it's clear that they live, how would I put it, quite well. They have a big, beautiful home in a gated community, they both drive Mercedes, and the last time I was there they had a new boat in the driveway."

"They can't afford that on a non-profit salary, that's for sure," Martha laughed. "Maybe they have family money, or the husband makes a good income?" Martha continued, uncomfortable with the insinuation that was becoming obvious.

"Quisás," said Ruth, shaking her head. "Her husband says he's a business consultant, but it's kind of a running joke that no one knows what he really does."

"Well," said Martha, "regardless of their personal situation, there's going to be an impact on the non-profit community. Even the appearance of impropriety can send funders running. Julia, can you let me know if any information is being shared on the CCS message board, of if a meeting has been scheduled to address this?"

"Absolutely" said Julia, as she folded up the paper and handed it to Ruth.

Later that month, Martha met with Carlene at a local coffee shop. As chair of the agency's board, Carlene had overseen the 360 evaluation process for Martha's annual review. Over the past few weeks, Carlene had solicited feedback from staff, clients, and current and former board members about Martha's performance in a variety of areas, and now she had a summary to share with Martha.

"Well, Martha," Carlene began, "I think by and large, you'll be happy with the results of your evaluation. I'm particularly pleased with the response we had from the staff and the clients who took the time to complete the surveys and provide comments."

Martha was just as curious about the results as she was about the effectiveness of the process. "I've heard criticism that staff are not as open and honest about their supervisors using the 360, but I hope that's not the case here," she said. "I'd like to think I've created an environment where people feel safe enough to tell the truth."

Carlene had read about those same concerns, which was why they had used an anonymous instrument using Survey Monkey and summarized comments rather than sharing them verbatim. "We really wanted some honest opinions, Martha, and I think the results show we were able to get some really good feedback."

Carlene handed Martha the summary document for her to review. "Go ahead and read it over while I look over the pie selections," she shared, making a funny show of putting the menu in front of her face.

As Martha read, she found themes that were familiar from previous evaluations of her work, though the format was different from previous assessments. Martha's staff and the agency's clients who participated found her to be supportive and helpful, a creative thinker and problem-solver, and a leader, modeling for everyone how to handle crises and everyday unexpected setbacks that often occur in social services. These qualities were important to Martha, and she prided herself on being a responsive director that took care of staff and clients. One example cited by both a client and a staff member that particularly pleased Martha was when Melissa had to be out on leave to care for her partner. Although Melissa and her partner were not legally married in their state and therefore not eligible for Family and Medical Leave, Martha allowed Melissa to take sick leave with pay and also covered her caseload while she was out. Clients only knew that Melissa had to be out for a week but found no disruption in their services with the switch to Martha as their temporary caseworker.

Carlene peered over her menu as Martha read the more critical section of the report.

"How are you feeling so far?" she inquired. Martha was so lost in her reading that she was startled when Carlene spoke.

"There's feedback here that I never dreamed I'd see, but not for the reasons you might think," she replied.

"After what's been going on with Patty Ortiz at The Children's Corner, the comments about my handling of the budget are particularly striking," Martha continued.

Carlene too had been surprised to see more than one person offer Martha "constructive criticism" about her openness with staff over the budget and in seeking their input into the development of the overall agency budget.

"I know you often use the staff when creating a budget for a grant or a new program, Martha, but it seems that the staff would like to be more informed about the overall budget," Carlene responded. "Especially the annual budget planning."

"To be honest, I have mixed feelings about this," Martha shared. "On the one hand, part of me would be happy to be more open about our finances and include the staff in annual budgeting. The other side of me, however, is really worried about maintaining morale since I am ultimately responsible for making cuts if needed and determining salaries, raises, etc." Martha had never considered changing the way she dealt with the financial concerns of the agency, but now she was questioning her approach.

"Well, here's how I see it," Carlene began. "There are privacy concerns about salaries, raises, etc. based on an individual's experience and work performance. From my perspective, those things should be private and only under your purview in consultation with the board. I do think, however, that there is room to be more inclusive of the entire staff in reviewing the budget each year, soliciting ideas for growth or cuts in programs, and consulting with staff on the quarterly reports you give to us at board meetings." Carlene went on, "It also sounds as though the staff really appreciate your ability to find a variety of funding sources to support the agency. In that sense, your handling of the budget is a real strength. You do such a good job of diversifying our funding streams that it protects the agency from some of the volatility that other non-profits face."

"Thanks," Martha said with a smile. "I guess I've approached the whole budget and financial piece from a different vantage point, and it's left staff with a sense that I'm either being secretive or too controlling. Neither one makes me happy," she said with a soft chuckle. "I think with the news about The Children's Corner and with the way non-profits are struggling right now, the more open I can be, the better."

"Let's keep talking about how to proceed, and we can discuss this with the board at our next meeting," Carlene said. "I suspect we'll get differing opinions about what information to share with staff and even how to approach discussions about the annual budget, but the more minds we get to work on this, the better."

Martha thanked Carlene for all her support and for helping her think through next steps. As they walked out to their cars, Martha shared how glad she was that they used this new process for evaluation. "I'm not sure I would have received this type of input if we hadn't chosen to do the 360 evaluation," she declared.

"Just keep in mind that this is a really good evaluation, Martha," Carlene said in an assuring tone. "Overall, the staff see you as incredibly competent, approachable, and supportive. But there are things that will be shared in an anonymous survey that are not likely to be said face to face. It's just human nature, I guess."

When Martha returned to her office she began to map out a plan for the next financial report so that the financial health of the agency could be shared with everyone. She also began jotting down ideas for including staff in budget development. She harkened back to her master's of social work program and a course she took in organizational management. It's easy to stray from best practices in the day-to-day operations of an agency, she thought to herself. I just take for granted that people trust me and my decisions and sometimes forget they are anxious about their jobs being cut or just simply want to feel that they are being heard.

She remembered the technique of zero based budgeting and wondered how her staff might respond if she got them all together and started from scratch on the budget for next year. When this technique is used, nothing is sacred or assumed to be necessary for continuation. It can be a scary process for staff, but it also forces everyone to consider how their roles fit with the agency's mission. It also challenges staff to review how they do things within programs and examine if there are more efficient and effective ways of providing services.

I'll run this idea by the board and see what they think, Martha thought as she closed her computer screen.

Over dinner, Martha shared the evaluation feedback with Allen.

"Honey, what I love most about you is that you really listen to what others have to say," Allen said after hearing Martha describe some changes she had planned as a result of staff feedback. "I've had any number of supervisors over the years that couldn't deal with *any* criticism. I've seen folks be retaliated against for simply asking a question about decisions that had been made. In my totally objective opinion, you're the best boss anyone could ask for."

Martha smiled and gave him a big hug. "Well, since I'm the best boss ever, I guess you'll be doing the dishes tonight?"

December 2007

On a crisp Monday morning, Martha retrieved the morning paper from her driveway. As the sun was beginning to rise, she noticed that her neighbor's house was still empty, the leafless trees and overgrown lawn standing as symbols of an economy in retreat. The headlines in the paper said it all. One predicted a dire holiday spending season as overburdened consumers wrestled with debt, and another questioned if Democratic presidential candidates would suggest tax policies to stimulate a lagging economy.

On the way to work Martha stopped at the post office to mail Jessie a care package of hot cocoa and chocolate chip cookies to help her get through finals. She was looking forward to having the kids home again for the holidays, though she knew their schedules would keep them busy. Brandon had been unsuccessful as a walk-on, but the basketball coach had been so impressed with his hustle and enthusiasm that he had asked him to be one of the team managers. Brandon was already talking about the holiday tournament on the East Coast that would allow him to spend New Year's Eve in New York City. Martha tried to console herself with the idea that her independent children were demonstrating a healthy transition to early adulthood, but she couldn't shake the feeling that they had grown up too fast.

As she entered her office Martha could see the voicemail message light blinking on her phone. After getting a pot of coffee started in the small staff kitchen, she sat down and played the message.

"Hi Martha, this is Annabelle Barr from CSSR. I have some important news to discuss with you. Please call me back as soon as possible." Dr. Barr was the evaluator from the Center for Social Service Research who had given the Helping Hands welfare-to-work program a glowing rating a few months earlier. She had left her cell phone number as well as her office number at the university, so Martha knew it must be important and out of the ordinary. Dr. Barr typically scheduled her evaluation visits at six-month intervals and usually did so over email. As it was still before eight, Martha made a note to call her at 9 a.m.

Martha heard voices and made her way to the lobby. Ruth and Melissa had just arrived and were talking about movies they wanted to see.

"I saw a trailer for the new Will Smith film called *I Am Legend*," said Melissa. "It looks kind of creepy but cool."

"What's it about?" asked Ruth, already skeptical of the answer she was about to receive.

"Like, the end of the world, and Will Smith is the only one alive, and he has to fight off these mutant creatures . . ."

"Basta ya!" said Ruth, waving her hand in front of her face.

"Sounds like something Allen and the twins are going to want to see," said Martha, chuckling at Ruth's response.

"Is that the guy from that TV show, what did they call it . . .?" asked Ruth.

" 'The Fresh Prince of Bel-Air,' " said Melissa immediately.

"Yes, that's it!" said Ruth. "While I was still teaching, I asked my students if they could all sing a song together. I was trying to make the point that music didn't bring people together as it had when I was growing up. And you know what they all started singing? The theme song from that show! I had never even seen an episode!"

Before she had even finished Melissa started to playfully sing the song ("In West Philadelphia, born and raised, on the playground was where I spent most of my days . . .").

"Fíjate, pues," said Ruth, shaking her head as Melissa playfully followed her down the hall to her office singing the tune.

MARTHA FINDS BABY CLOTHES FOR MRS. BILLINGS' GRANDCHILD...

Martha heard the front door open and saw a familiar face. Mrs. Billings had been a health care aide at a local assisted living facility but had thrown her back out lifting patients. For the last year she had been wrangling with the Social Security Administration in her attempt to receive disability benefits. Martha usually saw her toward the end of the month when her food stamp benefits ran out and she needed assistance from the Helping Hands pantry.

It flashed through Martha's mind that since this was the beginning of the month she might be having problems with her food stamps eligibility.

"Hello, Mrs. Billings. How are you?" Martha asked purposely.

"Going along to get along," said Mrs. Billings in response, shifting her cane so she could shake Martha's hand. "I know what you're thinking, but I'm not here for the food pantry."

"Oh, okay," said Martha. "Then how can we help you?"

"Well, I went to The Children's Corner yesterday to see if I could pick up some diapers and baby clothes for my granddaughter, but there was a sign on the door that said it was closed and would no longer be offering services."

"Really?" said Martha, conveying her surprise at the news.

"I've been reading stuff in the paper about it, but the last article I read made a point of saying that essential services would continue," said Mrs. Billings, clearly upset about her unexpected discovery of the agency's closure.

Covering her surprise, Martha shifted the conversation back to a more helpful space. "I'm not sure we have any diapers at the moment, but let's see if we can find some suitable baby clothes for you."

It was a few minutes after nine when Martha finished with Mrs. Billings. On the way back to her office she made a mental note that Helping Hands might want to consider filling the service gap, in whatever way possible, that was now open as a result of the closing of The Children's Corner. The community response to the closing of the agency would certainly be a hot topic at the CCS meeting that was scheduled for the next day. As Mrs. Billings had noted, the newspapers had continued to follow the story about The Children's Corner, and it was beginning to sound like a daytime soap opera. According to what Martha could piece together from the various articles, problems started when a state auditor noticed that the accountant listed by The Children's Corner was not authorized to do audits of non-profit organizations. When the state auditor contacted the executive director, she claimed it had been an honest mistake and, in an effort to save money, had authorized grad students from the local university accounting department to conduct the audit.

The story took a bizarre turn a couple of months later. The executive director, while waiting to meet state auditors at The Children's Corner office, left to retrieve some documents she said had been left at home. No one had seen or heard from her since. Shortly after her disappearance the media got wind of the story, and now the headlines at the River City *Gazette* routinely carried some new salacious detail about the executive director's financial transgressions. To Martha's knowledge, the staff had made a valiant effort to continue offering basic services, but apparently the fallout was just too much.

Before returning to her office Martha went to the break room and poured herself a cup of coffee. Her staff often joked about her caffeine habit, and one staff member had given her a giant coffee cup as a present that said "In a former life . . . I lived in Seattle." Settling down at her desk, Martha called Dr. Barr using the cell phone number she had provided.

The call was answered on the first ring. "Hello, this is Annabelle."

"Hi, Annabelle, this is Martha White from Helping Hands."

"Hi, Martha, thanks for getting back in touch with me so quickly."

"Absolutely," said Martha, "your message sounded urgent."

"Well, it is," replied Annabelle, in a tone that caused Martha instant consternation. She wondered if it had anything to do with the ongoing issues related to The Children's Corner. "I'm afraid I've received some bad news from DHS."

The Department of Human Services was the arm of state government that had funded the welfare-to work programs Martha and Helping Hands had been running for about three years.

"I'm all ears," replied Martha, keeping her response short in an effort to not betray her concern.

"Well," said Annabelle, "DHS has a new division chief who has a reputation for being a budget hawk. She called me in to talk about the welfare-to-work projects, but it was pretty clear from the start that she wants to give all the programs the axe."

"I'm really sorry to hear that," Martha replied, shaking her head at the news. "I thought after the sterling evaluation we received in your last report that we would be on solid footing."

"I would think so too," replied Annabelle, "especially since the money has already been apportioned by the legislature. But she completely dismissed most of my findings."

"Really?" said Martha, not even attempting to hide her surprise. "Even the findings about the high levels of starting pay for our program graduates?"

"I brought that up, for yours and a couple of other programs," responded Annabelle quickly, "but she dismissed them out of hand because they were based on 'self-report' by the clients served."

"Well, a lot of survey information is based on self-report!" exclaimed Martha while leaning back in her chair and shaking her head. "She might as well dismiss most of what the Census Bureau does."

"Don't I know it," affirmed Annabelle. "It was a really odd meeting. I was caught between defending the evaluation techniques and advocating for the programs themselves."

"It sounds like her mind was made up," said Martha.

"I'd say it was," said Annabelle, "but I was able to get her to agree to meet with a few of the executive directors of what I think are the best programs."

"I'm surprised she was even willing to do that," replied Martha, inwardly feeling a spark of hope for her program that was missing just a moment before.

"Quite frankly, I am too. And that's the real purpose of this call. I would like you and a few other executive directors to go to the capitol and meet with her. My hope is that you can persuade her of the good work you are doing and save funding for at least a few of the programs."

"Absolutely," said Martha. "I would be happy to do that."

"Unfortunately," replied Annabelle in a somewhat dejected tone, "I don't think the trip would be a reimbursable expense from the contract."

"That's fine," said Martha without hesitation, "I'm certainly willing to come at my own expense. Just let me know a potential date and I'll clear my schedule."

"I appreciate your willingness to do so. The other executive directors I've talked to have all said the same thing. I guess that's why you all run such good programs."

Martha thanked Dr. Barr for her efforts to salvage funding for the programs and hung up the phone. She looked at her December schedule and noticed that there was only one day—the holiday silent auction and fundraiser—that she couldn't miss, and that was scheduled for a Saturday. Martha couldn't help but think about the dire consequences if DHS eliminated the welfare-to-work grant. It was the largest contract Helping Hands operated, and the funds paid for part of her and Ruth's salary and all of Melissa's salary. Martha had worked with Melissa since she was an undergraduate social work intern and shuddered at the thought of losing her and the grant. The funds also paid for partial salaries of two River City Community College staff. It didn't make sense to Martha for effective programs with dedicated lines of funding to be cut, but she knew that non-profit funding could be unstable. It just added insult to injury that cuts too often took place when the need was greatest.

As she thought about what she might say to the DHS administrator, the ring of her office phone startled her. "This is Martha," she answered, "how can I help you?"

"Hey Martha," Julia began, "there's someone from the mayor's office on line 1. Should I patch it through?"

"Yes, of course," Martha replied. The phone immediately rang; Martha hit the button on her phone for line 1 and gave her usual greeting.

"Hello, Martha, this is Nancy Davis, administrative assistant to Mayor Thompson. Can you take a call from the mayor at this time?"

"Yes, certainly," Martha replied without hesitation.

Martha had met the mayor on several occasions at community events but wasn't entirely sure he would have remembered her from those brief encounters. Mayor Thompson had made a great deal of money from high-tech investments in the 1990s and had largely self-funded his campaign. Martha remembered that he and the city council had engaged in some high-profile scuffles lately, with the mayor seeking significant tax abatements to lure large businesses to River City.

The voice on the other end was vaguely familiar. "Hi, Martha, this is Bill Thompson. Thank you for taking my call."

"Certainly, Mr. Mayor, how can I help you?" Martha replied.

"Martha, you are no doubt aware of the ongoing situation with The Children's Corner?"

"Yes, I am, Mayor Thompson. It's a very unfortunate situation."

"Martha, I think you know that I have always been a stalwart supporter of the work that the non-profit sector does for this community."

"Yes, Mr. Mayor, I believe we have met at several community events and fundraisers."

"That's right. And one of the first things I did after the campaign was urge my wife to accept a position on the board of The Children's Corner. You know, she's a nurse practitioner by training and has always had a soft spot in her heart for kids."

Martha couldn't gauge the mayor's true regard for the non-profit community, but non-profit colleagues had told her that his wife Anne was a tireless advocate for worthy causes.

"At any rate," the mayor continued, "The board of The Children's Corner has decided to file a civil suit against the former director, *en absentia*, for the money that has gone missing, and the county DA has told me that she plans to file multiple indictments against her for tampering with government records. My wife Anne has recused herself from any further board decisions but it's clearly in everyone's best interests for me to pursue a resolution to this matter."

"That sounds like a wise decision, Mr. Mayor."

"Thank you, Martha," he replied, though barely pausing for breath. "I don't want people thinking that because of Anne's position that I don't want to get to the bottom of this. That's why 'd like to set up a committee to investigate the matter. Now I've asked around, and your name came up several times as someone who could be trusted to lead the inquiry."

"Really?" said Martha, unable to contain her surprise.

"That's right," said the mayor in a matter-of-fact tone. "Now, I'm not talking any sort of criminal investigation, just an inquiry into how this situation was allowed to happen and what can be done to keep things like this from happening again."

"Well, I'm flattered at the recommendation, Mr. Mayor," Martha began, "but I would have to think about the implications of this sort of responsibility on my work at Helping Hands and—"

"That's just the thing," the mayor interrupted. "I'd like to announce you as the commission chair tomorrow at the CCS meeting. We don't have a lot of time to sit on this."

Martha knew she was being pushed to make a quick decision. Her thoughts instantly flashed to one of her graduate policy courses with Dr. Gault and a tape recording he had played of President Lyndon Johnson in 1964 offering the leadership of the War on Poverty to an obviously overwhelmed and reluctant Sargent Shriver, who at the time was also the head of the Peace Corps.

"Well, if my board approves it, I guess I would consider—"

"That's great!" the mayor interjected. "I'll have Nancy share the details with you, and I'll see you tomorrow at the meeting. I knew I could count on you, Martha!"

Before she knew it, the administrative assistant was back on the phone letting Martha know that she would email a PDF file with the commission's instructions later that afternoon.

At home that evening with Allen, Martha picked at her food and pondered her next steps. As she expected, the board had given their approval for her to act as the commission chair. She had also taken the opportunity to alert them to the possibility of the welfare-to-work grant being cut. Martha had experienced staff leaving the agency, but it was typically voluntary or a result of a grant ending its funding cycle, not being cut midstream. She assured Allen that her lack of appetite had nothing to do with his cooking and, after the table was cleared, wrote down a list of non-profit leaders that she would like to serve with her on the commission.

The following morning, Martha arrived early at the United Way building where the CCS meeting was being held. She was delighted to see Alice Chan in attendance. Alice was the first name on her list, a former accounting executive who was now the director of the Chinese Community Center. Martha knew her training and experience would be invaluable in following the trail of financial wrongdoing that was alleged to have occurred. As she made her way to speak with Alice, a woman in a blue power suit stepped in front of her.

"Hello, Martha, I'm Nancy Davis, assistant to the mayor. We spoke on the phone yesterday. Could you please come with me? The mayor would like to speak with you before the meeting begins."

Nancy led Martha out of the large room and down a nearby hallway where Mayor Thompson was waiting with his wife, Anne.

"Hi, Martha," said Mayor Thompson, "this is my wife Anne."

Martha recognized her from previous social engagements and noted that she seemed to have a kindness to her that was juxtaposed to her husband's brusque manner. "Nice to meet you," she said.

"Martha, I really appreciate you taking the lead on this. The darn thing is, I just learned this morning that the executive director may have embezzled money from other sources as well. We're obviously dealing with a criminal outlier here, but the whole non-profit sector is going to get a black eye if we don't set the record straight as soon as possible."

"I completely agree, Mr. Mayor, and I've already put together a list of potential commission members that I think—"

"That's great, Martha. Whatever you think is best. But the sheer size of this larceny suggests that this is a system-wide failure of oversight, not the fault of any individual."

Martha couldn't help but think that the reference was to the mayor's wife and her role as a board member of The Children's Corner.

"Obviously," Martha replied, "the commission should look at the agency's oversight mechanisms but also community-level steps that can be taken to minimize this sort of behavior."

"Absolutely," replied the mayor enthusiastically.

"And I would just like to say that I will be happy to answer any questions you may have about my role on the board and our interactions with Patty over these last few years. I mean, I'm still shocked at the whole thing," added Anne somewhat uncomfortably.

"I appreciate that," said Martha, touching her on the arm gently.

The mayor's assistant signaled to them from down the hall that the meeting was about to start.

"Well, shall we?" said the mayor to Martha and Anne as they headed down the hall.

Martha couldn't help but think that 2007 was going out with a bang.

Discussion Questions

1. Based upon what you read about the financial impropriety at The Children's Corner in River City, what do you believe is the role of a board of directors in maintaining oversight of executive directors of agencies? Who should have access to financial information and funds within an agency's staffing structure?

2. What would you do as a director to insure that funds collected were appropriately allocated and there was sound financial management for your agency?

3. What impacts would the entire non-profit community potentially face if such a case were to happen in your community?

4. Martha receives the results of her 360-degree evaluation from her staff in this chapter. What are the strengths and weaknesses of using this type of evaluation? What would you do in Martha's place to address the issues raised by her staff?

5. Agencies relying on grant funding often face cuts due to political changes at the federal and state levels. In our story, the state office brought in a person whose primary role was to cut budgets and save money. What is your opinion about cutting successful programs in the face of limited funds in state budgets? What processes would you use as a budget director to make decisions about spending?

Potential Assignments

1. Have students talk to three different agency directors about the role their boards of directors play in setting budgets, overseeing finances, and evaluating the director. Report back to class and design a model structure for appropriate oversight of the agency by the board.

2. Research the 360-degree evaluation method. Have students compare it to other forms of staff evaluation they find via agency contacts in the community and online. What are the strengths and weaknesses of each method?

3. Budget development exercise: Using the concept of zero-based budgeting, have students create an agency budget for a fictional agency of the professor's design. They are to imagine a required 10% cut to the grant funding that supports the agency. Give them some basic data about success of each program in the agency via evaluation and provide funds allocated by program. This will require construction of a budget or using a sample budget from an existing agency. Have them discuss in small groups and report back their process of decision-making regarding budget cuts.

Suggested Readings

Bell, Jeanne, Masaoka, Jan, & Zimmerman, Steve. (2010). *Nonprofit sustainability: Making strategic decisions for financial viability.* San Francisco: Jossey-Bass.

Carroll, Deborah, & Stater, Keely Jones. (2009). Revenue diversification in nonprofit organizations: Does it lead to financial stability? *Journal of Public Administration Research and Theory, 19*(4), 947–966.

Davis, Carl. (2013). *Tax incentives: Costly for states, drag on the nation.* Institute on Taxation and Economic Policy. Retrieved from http://www.itep.org/pdf/taxincentiveeffectiveness.pdf

Gordon, Tracy. (2012, December). *State and local budgets and the Great Recession.* Stanford, CA: Stanford Center on Poverty and Inequality. Retrieved from: https://web.stanford.edu/group/recessiontrends/cgi-bin/web/sites/all/themes/barron/pdf/StateBudgets_fact_sheet.pdf

Jones, Richard. (2007, September 19). In Louisiana, a tree, a fight, and a question of justice. *New York Times.* Retrieved from http://www.nytimes.com/2007/09/19/us/19jena.html?_r=0

Sontag-Padilla, Lisa, Staplefoote, Lynette, & Gonzalez Morganti, Kristy. (2012). *Financial sustainability for non-profit organizations: A review of the literature.* Santa Monica, CA: Rand Corporation. Retrieved from http://www.rand.org/content/dam/rand/pubs/research_reports/RR100/RR121/RAND_RR121.pdf

State budgeting and lessons learned from the economic downturn: Analysis and commentary from state budget officers. (2013, Summer). National Association of State Budget Officers. Retrieved from https://www.nasbo.org/sites/default/files/State%20Budgeting%20and%20Lessons%20Learned%20from%20the%20Economic%20Downturn-final.pdf

Story, Louise. (2012, December 1). As companies seek tax deals, governments pay high price. *New York Times.* Retrieved from http://www.nytimes.com/2012/12/02/us/how-local-taxpayers-bankroll-corporations.html?pagewanted=all

3

Change Is Coming

January 2008

Martha returned from the New Year holiday ready to begin work on the commission. She had spoken to Alice Chan and was grateful that she had accepted the offer to help lead the investigation. The first problem they encountered was finding contact information for former employees. Setting Julia to the task, Martha decided to begin by interviewing all the members of The Children's Corner board. Martha knew that the investigation could be an enormous time drain if she wasn't careful and resolved to work as efficiently as possible, limiting the inquiry to a search for facts and basing recommendations on widely accepted best practices.

Martha was also looking forward to joining Dr. Barr in a meeting with the new Department of Human Services (DHS) director. She hoped that she and the other executive directors would be able to convince the DHS official that the welfare-to-work programs were worth keeping and that the employment-related services that they provided were in line with the work-oriented goals that had caused President Clinton to sign the historic welfare reform legislation in 1996.

Sitting in her office with the door open, Martha could hear some clients in the lobby debating the upcoming national championship game between Louisiana State and Ohio State. Though Martha was not much of a football fan, she had volunteered to host a game watch for Allen and his co-workers. The phone rang while she was thinking of take-out options that she could pick up after work.

Julia was on the other end. "Hi, Martha, Dr. Barr is on line 1. Should I patch her through?"

"Yes, of course." Martha was expecting a call from Dr. Barr to discuss the logistics of the meeting, but as soon as she heard her voice she knew something was wrong. Dr. Barr wasted no time on pleasantries.

"Hi, Martha, I'm really sorry to have to share this, but I just got off the phone with the director. She has not only decided to cancel our meeting but she is going to cut *all* the programs."

Martha leaned back in her chair and looked up at the ceiling as she heard the news. She had hoped, along with other program directors, to have a chance to plead her case, but now even that slim hope was gone. "Obviously, her mind was already made up," Martha replied with an air of resignation.

"I'm really sorry, Martha. The whole conversation took less than five minutes. I'm honestly at a loss . . ."

"It's not your fault, Annabelle. You went out of your way to salvage what you could, and I really appreciate all that you have done to advocate for the programs."

"It's just so frustrating, you know?" Dr. Barr quickly responded. "I spent years in grad school learning about research, and how to make welfare policy more effective, but it seems that the state bureaucracy is just not interested in what really works."

Martha had spent years in the non-profit sector and completely understood the sentiment that Dr. Barr was expressing, but with so much on her plate she didn't see the need to perseverate on the decision. Instead, she pressed Dr. Barr for details. "Did she say when she planned to terminate funding for the programs?"

"All she said was that letters would be sent to each program."

Ten days later Martha received a letter stating that all funding for the welfare-to-work program would cease on March 15.

February 2008

In February, the prospect of having to make serious cuts to the budget and reduce the number of staff was becoming a depressing reality. Martha and Carlene met to discuss options for new revenue.

"I wonder if we can capitalize on all the experience we both have in child welfare, Carlene," asked Martha. She and Carlene were meeting at their favorite neighborhood coffee shop near Martha's home in River City.

"I have asked myself the same question," Carlene responded. "It certainly feels as though we need to broaden our focus. I guess they don't say 'programs for the poor are poor programs' for nothing."

Martha shared a story with Carlene from her college days. "I remember Professor Gault saying that the way a country or state uses its resources is a direct reflection of how it feels about certain populations. Social Security has done a great job reducing the number of elderly who live in poverty, and now it's so popular that even conservative politicians don't want to mess with it."

"President Bush learned that lesson the hard way, if I remember correctly," interjected Carlene, a reference to the "town hall" meetings President Bush held after his reelection in 2004 that unsuccessfully sought to privatize all or part of Social Security.

"Right!" agreed Martha. "That was a disaster. It's just too bad that children don't have their own social security program!"

"Well, we do spend a good deal of money on the child welfare system, don't we?" asked Carlene in response.

"Yes, but too often only after the damage has been done," replied Martha, shaking her head. It was an allusion to their shared experience working in the child welfare system. "We should stress prevention, not just damage control."

"True enough," Carlene soberly replied. "So where does that leave us? Do you have any good leads on funding?"

"I've been looking into some discretionary grants from the Administration for Children and Families (ACF)," Martha began. "At first I thought we might be able to partner with the university on Title-IV E funds for training of staff, but if we have to put up matching funds to participate, it's just not possible. I'm doubtful that the state would put up a match for us. So I started exploring some discretionary programs and found two sources that might be worth pursuing."

"Martha," Carlene said, putting down her coffee mug, "You never cease to amaze me. What programs look good?"

Martha sifted through some papers she brought with her. "The first one is called the Promoting Safe and Stable Families program. It focuses on working with at-risk families to prevent child abuse and neglect. The announcement says that proposals should seek to capitalize on the strengths and resources of the families and their communities. The guidelines also ask for community collaboration among agencies, and, thanks to the welfare-to-work program, we would have no problem documenting our ability to collaborate with other non-profits. I also like this program because it's prevention-based."

"No wonder prevention was on your mind!" Carlene exclaimed. It was clear that she was excited about this funding opportunity. "I would love to see Helping Hands get involved in prevention work! I never told you about this, but did you know that a young child was found buried in the woods recently?

"I do," said Martha. "What a horrible story! His mother's boyfriend killed him, right?"

"Yes," replied Carlene. "The autopsy showed he had multiple fractures that had never healed correctly. Poor baby must have suffered for years. We did all the flowers for his funeral. I worked with the grandparents on the arrangements. They had to deal with the loss of their grandson but also that their daughter didn't get him out of harm's way. They lived out-of-state and had been estranged from her for a number of years."

"I hadn't realized you were connected to it. It's just heartbreaking!" Martha said, shaking her head.

"Well, I'm still a social worker at heart, Martha, and I would really like to get involved in something that can prevent this sort of tragedy from happening again."

"Well, if we do pursue a prevention grant, we would need to partner with the nursing programs at the community college and the university. We could do a visiting nurse/social worker program for new parents," Martha said. "There's evidence that these types of programs reduce the incidence of child abuse and neglect and increase the likelihood of timely immunizations. I like the idea of having nurses and social workers teaming up."

"This sounds great," said Carlene while looking over the program description, "but before we go too far, what's the other option you found?"

"The other is an adoption grant program," Martha explained. "One of the goals of this program is to increase the rate of adoptions among minority children and youth in the foster care system. The goal is to design a program to recruit minority families and support them in adopting minority children. I really like this option too. Minority youth are overrepresented in the foster care system, and I think we could design a program that uses our community connections to recruit, train, and support potential adoptive families and help move these kids to permanency." Carlene pushed her glasses down her nose and began to read over the grant guidelines.

Martha was excited about both program options. She had met Carlene when they both worked as caseworkers in the foster care system and knew just how important finding a permanent family was for youth, especially those likely to age out of the system with no support. The statistics about foster youth described in the guidelines were dismal: high rates of high school dropout, homelessness, unemployment, and drug use, and college completion rates of less than 5%.

After reading about both of the grant opportunities Carlene contemplated the goodness-of-fit and funding potential for both programs. "Martha, I think we could add a mentoring option into either of these," she said. "I've been a volunteer with Big Brothers/Big Sisters, and while they are the most well-known program for mentoring in the country, their success with foster youth is limited. The model they use just doesn't seem to fit. Mentors would be a good option for new parents, especially if they don't have family or friends to provide support and advice. I think it would be a plus to either proposal to add a mentoring component."

Martha sipped her coffee and took a moment to think about Carlene's idea. "Honestly, Carlene, I'm having a hard time choosing which option to pursue, but regardless, I think you're right. A mentoring component would work really well with either group."

Carlene was clearly pleased with Martha's positive reaction. "When I think back to what I have been able to accomplish, going to college, working as a caseworker, starting my own business, even raising my kids, I've had mentors all along the way. I think new parents and foster kids would really benefit from that kind of a relationship. And research shows that people from social service backgrounds often make the best mentors."

Martha lit up upon hearing this information. "All the more reason to bring in the social work program as a partner. I guess my next step should be to connect with the nursing program directors at the community college and the university. I'm pretty sure that Dr. Gault or Dr. Barr would be willing to work with us, whatever direction we take. It wouldn't be hard to justify the need for social work interns in both programs. I also need to talk with Rev. Anderson; I think his church could be the starting point for recruitment of foster parents and maybe even mentors."

"And with the welfare-to-work grant ending, he might be happy to join us on another project," added Carlene. Martha nodded in agreement. "Sounds like the responses you get from those meetings will help us decide what to do."

"I think you're right," said Martha. "Maybe they will come down in favor of one program over another. I don't know."

"Well, either way, there's no time to waste," said Carlene while looking over the program guidelines. "Both of these grants are due in just over a month."

"Why does it always seem like these things get thrown together at the last minute?" Martha said, not really expecting an answer.

"I guess it's just the nature of the non-profit beast," added Carlene with a sigh.

A sudden look of dejection came over Martha's face. "It doesn't look like there's any way to avoid layoffs. Even if we're successful the new programs won't be funded until October, when the new federal budget year begins.

We can't maintain our staff until then without some other funds." Carlene nodded affirmatively, and Martha wondered if the ups and downs of the non-profit sector would ever get easier.

Ten days later, Martha briefed the board on her meetings with the college faculty, Rev. Anderson, and staff of the local DHS. Regardless of Martha's feelings about working with the very agency that was about to cut her welfare-to-work funding, she knew DHS assistance would be instrumental in any program they might start. The staff of DHS, while certainly interested in strengthening recruitment of foster families, believed the visiting nurse/social work prevention program was the best option for Helping Hands. They strongly encouraged Martha to pursue the grant and offered to assist with referrals. DHS could make referrals from cases where abuse or neglect had been alleged and could also make referrals from a fragile families study they were conducting in the local public hospital that identified births to young mothers, mothers with alcohol or drug issues, or mothers of non-native origin.

The faculty from the social work and nursing programs at both colleges were enthusiastic about the possibilities and immediately agreed to provide a variety of support to the program. Not only would they send students to be interns, but they also agreed to start co-instructed courses that both nursing and social work students would take in child abuse prevention and intervention. Dr. Gault had been researching the concept of inter-professional education, a relatively new movement within higher education, where social workers, nurses, doctors and other health professionals were trained together in teams and prepared to work as teams in health care settings. He felt Martha's prevention program was a perfect place for the university to begin their version of inter-professional education.

The career services offices at both schools could also assist in the recruitment of social workers and nurses for employment in the program. Martha believed she would need two full-time social workers and two full-time nurses, each sharing a caseload of fifteen to twenty families. She could maintain Melissa as one of the social workers and allow her to supervise social work interns each semester. Martha planned to rely on the nursing faculty to help find nurses who would enjoy this type of work and who believed in the collegial mission of the program. It was critical that everyone involved be comfortable sharing cases and collaborating with each other and the families referred to the program.

Immediately after putting the partners together, Martha began writing the grant. Dr. Gault and a member of the nursing faculty at the university agreed to write the needs assessment for the geographic area they planned to serve.

A DHS liaison provided data on referrals they received for clients needing prevention and early intervention services. Martha described in detail the lack of prevention services that existed in River City and the ways in which the proposed services would meet these needs. The proposal described how the referral process would work and the ways in which key partnerships in the community would support the program. She also included a mentoring component, with volunteers recruited from Rev. Anderson's church, that she hoped would set the program apart from other proposals that the ACF would receive from around the country. Finally, she wrote a justification for staffing needs and budget requests. She sent a draft of the proposal to her board and other program stakeholders, with a note that she hoped to receive feedback in time to make revisions before the grant was due. The grant was due in two weeks, and Martha had worked significant overtime to pull everything together on such short notice. It was exhausting work, but Martha believed the program could really benefit vulnerable families in River City and at the same time broaden the scope of expertise that Helping Hands could leverage in the community.

Having completed the rough draft of the grant proposal, Martha turned her attention to the investigation of financial wrongdoing and mismanagement that had taken place at The Children's Corner. Amazingly, new information kept coming to light. An official from the Association of Child Care Resource and Referral Agencies came forward to allege that the former director, who had served as a volunteer treasurer for the group, had likely stolen more than $150,000 over the previous six years. Articles in the *River City Star* included interviews with some of the fifteen former employees who had lost their jobs and detailed the impact on the community of the non-profit's closure. An email had circulated recently through the Council of Community Services (CCS) list-serve inquiring about the ability of other agencies to step up and provide the postpartum support groups, parenting classes, and childcare referrals that The Children's Corner would no longer be offering. There was even a question about what to do with the 13,000-volume lending library of books and educational materials that The Children's Corner had previously made available to clients, advocates, and educators.

With Alice at her side, Martha interviewed all the members of the advisory board. One point that quickly became apparent was the implicit trust that each member of the board had given to the director. Only one board member, a local business owner who had spent some time in the child welfare system as an adolescent, had asked to see financial statements, but his requests were politely rebuffed. Perceiving little support among the other board members, he dropped his requests rather than press the issue. It was clear that the board members had been influenced by the charisma of the former director and had put their energy and skills toward the fundraising and support activities that the director had sanctioned.

With Julia's help, Martha and Alice scheduled interviews with key staff members from The Children's Corner. Retrieving the paper in the morning before her first interview, Martha was astonished to read yet another salacious headline about the ongoing case. According to the article, the former director had first been hired by The Children's Corner as a bookkeeper—while she was on parole for previous theft charges! When she met with Alice later that morning at Helping Hands, it was the first thing they discussed.

"I just can't believe all the information that keeps coming out!" Martha exclaimed in an exasperated tone. "If I had known what I was getting myself into . . ."

"Or getting me into!" replied Alice with a grin.

"Right!" said Martha, somewhat sheepishly. "I guess misery loves company."

"Well, look at it this way," said Alice with a chuckle. "It makes one of the recommendations we can offer crystal clear: Do not hire executive directors who are on parole for felony larceny!"

Martha appreciated Alice's light-hearted gesture. "In social work, we would call that a 'positive reframe,'" she added. "But seriously," Martha continued, "the social work interns we hire at Helping Hands have to complete a background check, so it's hard for me to imagine that she was able to get as far as she did without her history being an issue."

"The social services are really unique," said Alice. "Unlike the business world, it's more of an ethic of compassion versus compensation. I think we give people the benefit of the doubt just for wanting to do the work. And, just like anywhere else, one bad decision can have huge implications."

Over the next week Martha and Alice finished interviewing former Children's Corner employees and found that the executive director had tightly managed all the budgetary information. Information from one of the employee interviews stood out. She told Martha and Alice that all the important budget information was on the executive director's laptop, which was password protected and which she took home every night. It was also clear that none of the employees had a sense of the overall budget picture of the agency or an understanding of the contractor relationships The Children's Corner maintained with other agencies and service providers. Investigating this information further, Alice discovered that the executive director had for

years been writing checks to a fictitious vendor and had probably also pock-
eted portions of receipts that should have been deposited in their entirety to
The Children's Corner account.

To Martha and Alice, a clear picture emerged. At practically every step of
the process, from the initial hiring to the day-to-day administration and oversight of grant and contract funds, important safeguards were missing. These
gaps left the agency at the mercy of a charismatic charlatan who played on
people's trust and exploited the good will of funders, employees, and board
members. Martha and Alice knew, however, that regardless of the reforms
they would suggest, the extent of the financial mismanagement they had
uncovered would negatively impact the non-profit sector in River City and
beyond.

The following week, Martha sat at her desk, a copy of the ACF home-
visit grant in front of her. I'm old-school, she thought to herself. I'll always
need a hard copy to look over. She was pleased with how well the grant had
come together and the quality of the separate sections that each member had
contributed. She was particularly pleased with the feedback she had received
from Robert, the new board member. He had suggested an alternative and
cleaner method of detailing the budget. Martha was grateful for the input,
and his effort showed that he was willing to go the extra mile to support
Helping Hands and its mission.

She submitted the proposal and hoped for the best, then turned her
attention to the layoffs taking place as a result of the termination of the
welfare-to-work grant. It was the least favorite part of her job, and a hazard
of non-profit work in general, but there was no time to waste. Martha knew
that more layoffs would be forthcoming if they did not procure new sources
of funding.

March 2008

Martha woke early on a weekend morning in March, surveyed a kitchen full
of empty pizza boxes and dirty dishes . . . and smiled. Jessie was home for
spring break and had invited some of her high school friends to stay the night.
Brandon had also come over with a few of his friends to watch some March
Madness basketball with Allen. After removing the pizza boxes, Martha sat
down to read the *New York Times*. She was surprised to read an article by
an op-ed columnist that a bailout of the US financial system was imminent.
She knew that the economy had been slowing down and had even read that
a recession was all but inevitable, but the tenor of the article was clear: the

US economy was facing a looming crisis, and, despite protestations to the contrary from Treasury Secretary Henry Paulson, a former Goldman Sachs chief executive, nothing short of a massive government bailout was necessary. It was a terrible time to lose program funding and reduce the number of staff.

Helping Hands had faced significant challenges over the past six months. In spite of their efforts to apply for grants, the loss of the welfare-to-work funds forced Martha to reduce Melissa to part-time, although she had convinced the board to draw from a contingency fund to continue her health insurance. Melissa added another part-time job to compensate for the loss in income but chose to keep her foot in the door and wait to see if the new program would be funded. She had worked with Martha since she was a social work student intern and was excited about the prospect of working with young, at-risk families. Martha also reduced Ruth to part-time and reduced her own salary by 10%. But the hardest part of losing the welfare-to-work grant was having to tell the vocational health sciences students at the college that they would no longer receive the financial and material support that the program offered. Indeed, within two weeks of the program closing, Martha heard that several students had reluctantly dropped out of the program for lack of resources. The uncertainty of non-profit funding was frustrating, but Martha took heart in the knowledge that they had helped many students during the program's operation, students who would go on to have long and productive careers in various health science fields.

May 2008

In May, Martha and Alice completed interviews with former staff and board members of The Children's Corner and put the final touches on the report that they were scheduled to submit to the mayor's office. The effort, which had taken place on top of the grant proposal and the day-to-day management of Helping Hands, had been exhausting but eye-opening. In addition to the interviews, Martha and Alice had researched best practices in non-profit account management, most of which had been missing from The Children's Corner. The research had often kept Martha reading late into the night, but the information proved quite valuable. Martha and Alice had discussed making a presentation to the CCS to discuss the findings and recommendations once the report had been made public.

Julia brought the mail into Martha's office and placed it on her desk.

"Here goes nothing," said Martha with a flourish as she attached the report in an email to the mayor's assistant.

"Is that the big mayor's report?" Julia asked. "Because it's hard keeping up with all the stuff you're doing these days."

Martha's phone rang almost immediately. "Hi, Martha, this is Nancy Davis, assistant to Mayor Thompson."

"Well, that was fast!" Martha joked in response.

"I know," Nancy answered in a matter-of-fact tone. "We were just discussing the press conference when you emailed, and I thought it best to share the details with you as soon as possible."

"Press conference?" Martha asked quizzically.

"Yes," Nancy replied quickly, "the mayor has scheduled a press conference for Friday morning to discuss your report. As you know, the national media has covered this story extensively, and Mayor Thompson wants people to know that he takes this problem seriously. The mayor would like to meet with you at 8:30 a.m. sharp, and the press conference will start at 9:00.

On Friday morning, after a brief meeting with Mayor Thompson, Martha and Alice faced a phalanx of reporters and photographers in the city hall press room. The mayor had counseled them to keep their remarks short and to the point. Martha took a deep breath and stepped up to the podium. "Non-profit organizations play a vital role in American democracy," she began, "because they serve as an intermediary institution between the government and the people. In their role as an advocate for vulnerable and disempowered groups, non-profit organizations can help to more efficiently meet basic human needs and push government to be more responsive to everyday citizens. Because of this important role, however, the philanthropic sector must wisely use the resources given to it by private donors and through government contracts. We believe that the trust that the public puts in non-profit organizations should be maintained through a maximum level of transparency and rigorous accounting and administrative safeguards."

Martha continued with a brief description of the problems they found and then introduced Alice, who discussed a list of recommendations for non-profit agencies to follow. Alice discussed the need for advisory board members to accept a financial oversight function and to retain auditors separate from the executive director. She also mentioned a system of internal controls to approve vendors on a yearly basis and create an accounting process so that no one person controlled checks written to or disbursed from the organization.

After the presentation, Martha and Alice answered several questions from reporters, but shortly after the questions and answer session began, Mayor Thompson interrupted. "I think we can all agree that the transgressions identified in this report are the result of one bad apple who took advantage of a trusting system. Furthermore, I have just been informed that Patti Ortiz, the former executive director of The Children's Corner, has been apprehended in the Dominican Republic and extradition proceedings will begin right away." Immediately, the media turned their attention to Mayor Thompson and information related to the arrest and extradition of the fugitive ex-director.

Alice leaned over and whispered in Martha's ear, "I think we just got scooped."

Discussion Questions

1. The chapter mentions that after the 2004 election President Bush conducted numerous Town Hall meetings to discuss reforms to the Social Security program, including privatizing all or part of the payroll contributions. Though his efforts were rebuffed, many young people do not feel that Social Security will be available when they reach retirement age. Why is this idea so prevalent among young people?
2. What is Title IV-E funding and how does it impact social workers and social work students?
3. Mentor programs like Big Brothers, Big Sisters are very popular, but the impact of mentor programs is often mixed. Have you ever been mentored or acted as a mentor? Describe some of the benefits you experienced. Were there any shortcomings in your experience?
4. The chapter discusses some best practices designed to increase financial transparency among non-profit organizations. Which reforms do you think would be the most difficult to implement? If you were asked to sit on the board of an organization that was not forthcoming with regard to its financial disclosures, what do you think would be the best course of action to take?

Suggested Readings

About the Fragile Families and Child Wellbeing Study. (n.d.). Princeton University/ Columbia University. Retrieved from http://www.fragilefamilies.princeton.edu/about

Ball, Andrea, & Dexheimer, Eric. (2010, April 22). Family connections: The death of a nonprofit. *Austin-American Statesman*. Retrieved from http://www.statesman. com/news/news/local/family-connections-the-death-of-a-nonprofit-1/nRr9p/

Carlson, Bob. (2011, January 12). Embezzlement happens: It's what charities do next that matters. *The Chronicle of Philanthropy*. Retrieved from: https://philanthropy. com/article/Embezzlement-Happens-Its/227795

Child welfare outcomes: 2009–2012. (2012). Report to Congress. US Department of Health and Human Services. Retrieved from http://www.acf.hhs.gov/sites/default/files/cb/cwo09_12.pdf

Children's Bureau. (n.d.). Title IV-E: Foster Care. Retrieved from http://www.acf.hhs.gov/programs/cb/resource/title-ive-foster-care

Freeth, Della Hammick, Marilyn, Reeves, Scott, Koppel, Ivan, & Barr, Hugh. (2005). *Effective interprofessional education: Development, delivery, and evaluation* (Promoting Partnership for Health). New York: Wiley-Blackwell.

Galston, William (2007, September 21). *Why the 2005 Social Security initiative failed, and what it means for the future.* Washington, DC: Brookings Institute. Retrieved from: http://www.brookings.edu/research/papers/2007/09/21governance-galston

Krugman, Paul. (2008, March 17). The B word. *New York Times.* Retrieved from: http://www.nytimes.com/2008/03/17/opinion/17krugman.html?_r=0

Rhodes, Jean. (2012). *Big Brothers Big Sisters' youth outcome report: Executive summary. Public/private ventures.* Retrieved from http://www.bbbs.org/atf/cf/%7B8778D05C-7CCB-4DEE-9D6E-70F27C016CC9%7D/012412_YOS_executive.pdf

Stoltzfus, Emilie. (2012). *Child Welfare: State Plan Requirements under the Title IV-E Foster Care, Adoption Assistance, and Kinship Guardianship Assistance Program.* Congressional Research Service. Retrieved from http://greenbook.waysandmeans.house.gov/sites/greenbook.waysandmeans.house.gov/files/2012/R42794_gb.pdf

The White House. (n.d.). Strengthening Social Security for future generations. Retrieved from https://georgewbush-whitehouse.archives.gov/infocus/social-security/youth/

What is the Administration for Children & Families? (n.d.). Retrieved from https://www.acf.hhs.gov/

4

History in the Making

On a mild June morning, Martha walked to the end of her driveway to pick up her paper. She looked down the block to the home of her former neighbors. Though the house had remained vacant for many months, she assumed that the home had finally been leased since the sign had come down and there was a car in the driveway. Looking the other way, Martha realized that it had been some time since she had seen the Johnsons walking through the neighborhood. She made a mental note to check in on them after work in the evening.

Opening the paper, she stared at the headlines. It read "Obama Has Enough Delegates to Clinch Nomination." Most Americans had first heard about Barack Obama when he gave an electrifying speech as an Illinois Senate candidate at the 2004 Democratic National Convention. But Martha had first heard of him while reading a book in the late 1990s by the former 1960s radical Bill Ayres called *A Kind and Just Parent*. The book was a description of Jane Addams' efforts to start a children's court in early twentieth-century Chicago and how nearly a century later juvenile justice in Chicago had become a national disgrace. In one chapter, the author described riding a bike through south Chicago *past the home of writer Barack Obama*. When Senator Obama announced his candidacy for the presidency in 2007 Martha was intrigued but thought it would be similar to the Republican presidential campaigns of African American Alan Keyes in 1996 and 2000 or Democrat Carol Moseley Braun in 2004, an interesting curiosity but one that wouldn't last.

But now it was really happening. Unlike other young Democratic Senators before him who had unsuccessfully jumped into presidential frays like John Edwards and Al Gore, Barack Obama and his message of hope had won the primary support of a broad coalition of Democratic voters against the experience and deep war chests of Senators Joe Biden and Hillary Clinton. Though his popularity was strongest amongst African Americans, with over 90% saying they would vote for him, he was also energizing young voters and using the Internet and new media techniques to great advantage. The coming campaign was going to be a study in contrasts: the first major party African American candidate, a charming junior senator still in his first term, against John McCain, a cranky Senator from Arizona with decades of Senate experience, known more for his voluble temper and his years as a Vietnam POW than his statesmanship. Like the rest of the country, Martha knew this was going to be a historic election with serious implications with regard to the economy, foreign policy, and, of course, a potentially powerful step forward for African Americans.

During the lunch hour at Helping Hands, Martha helped serve clients in the food pantry. Typically, demand for assistance from the pantry was lowest early in the month when food stamp benefits had been distributed and would pick up later in the month when food stamp benefits had been expended. But larger numbers of people had been showing up to receive assistance over the past few months. Martha didn't know if the increase in the number of clients seeking food stamps assistance was related to the Farm Bill that had just been signed that allowed for a temporary increase in benefit levels. She had long suspected that demand for food aid was a harbinger of the economy's health, but it was becoming difficult to serve the number of people seeking assistance with a depleted staff. After working in the pantry for two hours, it was clear that many of the people seeking assistance were recently unemployed, and many had no experience seeking food stamps, or what was now referred to as Supplemental Nutrition Assistance Program (SNAP) assistance.

As a Child Protective Services caseworker early in her career, Martha had helped many families apply for food stamps assistance, and she knew that the application was long and complicated. The application in many states was coupled with information needed to ascertain eligibility for other programs like Temporary Assistance for Needy Families, Medicaid, and children's health programs. Though this reduced the need to complete multiple applications, filling out the required information and providing the requisite documentation could be a daunting task. The arduous nature of the food stamps application and the stigma associated with receiving benefits were the primary reasons why millions of eligible people did not apply for benefits. Regardless, Martha knew that food pantry resources could not substitute for the tens of billions of dollars distributed by the food stamp program every year and decided to train her meager staff and volunteers to help people apply for food stamp benefits.

A week later, Martha sat at the dinner table with Jessie while Allen and Brandon did the dishes. The kids were spending a few weeks at home before heading out for the rest of the summer. Jessie was beginning an internship in Washington, D.C., with her local legislator and Brandon was set to take two summer courses in physical therapy at Northern Arizona University. Listening to the kids go at each other in their usual way, Martha let out a gasp and shook her head.

"What's the matter?" asked Jessie.

"I just remembered that I had been meaning to check on Mr. and Mrs. Johnson down the street. I haven't seen them in a while," replied Martha. "Would you like to come with me?"

Brandon couldn't help himself. "I wouldn't do it, Jess. It's probably going to be one of those situations where she does nothing but tell stories about 'the olden times.' You could be trapped there for days." Jessie rolled her eyes in response and agreed to join Martha.

A few minutes later Martha and Jessie were sitting on a sofa in the Johnson's small but elegant living room. Mr. Johnson was listening to a baseball game in a nearby room.

"Can I get you something, some sweet tea perhaps?" asked Mrs. Johnson.

"No, thank you," replied Martha, "we just finished dinner. We really just came by to see how you and Mr. Johnson are doing."

"Oh, honey, we have been having ourselves a time of it, and I just don't know what to do," Mrs. Johnson sighed as she sat down in a chair on the other side of the coffee table.

"Well, I'm all ears if you don't mind sharing," said Martha.

"Me too," piped in Jessie as she moved to the edge of her seat. Martha knew that Jessie's willingness to listen would serve her well in the legislative internship she was about to begin.

Mrs. Johnson looked at them both for a moment and folded her hands across her lap. "Then if you don't mind," she said with just a hint of reservation, "I'd like to provide a little background."

"That would be fine," Martha answered.

"When I think about the situation we are in now, I can't help but think it really started in 1940, the year I was born. You see, my daddy had his land stolen from him in Mississippi, and rather than go back to sharecropping, he and Mama decided to seek a new life in Chicago. I was born a month after they arrived."

Martha knew immediately that Mrs. Johnson and her family had been part of the Great Migration, the movement of millions of African Americans from the deep south starting in World War I and continuing for decades after World War II.

Mrs. Johnson continued. "My parents thought they had found a more enlightened place, but they quickly found that Chicago had its own ways of keeping Black folks down."

"Was it just as bad as Mississippi?" asked Jessie, clearly intrigued with the way the story was unfolding.

"I wouldn't say that, honey," replied Mrs. Johnson. "When I was fifteen a boy I went to school with named Emmett Till was lynched when he went to visit family in Mississippi."

"You went to school with Emmett Till?" Martha asked, incredulous at the history that Mrs. Johnson was sharing.

"Yes, I did," she replied in a matter-of-fact tone, "but that's a story for another day."

Martha regained her composure. "Of course," she said. "Sorry to interrupt."

"No problem, honey" said Mrs. Johnson. "I just want to finish this story before the ball game ends. I don't want to upset Mr. Johnson anymore, because the man is already beside himself with worry."

It was clear that the Johnsons were having a serious problem, and Martha made a mental note to let Mrs. Johnson tell her story with a minimum of questions.

"My daddy got a job in a factory, and after a few years he decided that it would be better to own a home than continue paying rent for a ramshackle apartment. So my parents bought a house, or at least they thought they did. Turns out, they had only bought the house on contract."

The quizzical looks on Martha and Jessie's face spoke volumes.

"You see, buying a house on contract meant you didn't really own the place, but you weren't renting either. And if you missed one payment, well, according to the contract, they could kick you out, and you would lose all your money. This is what happened to my parents."

Martha was familiar with the way in which the Federal Housing Administration had refused loans to African Americans after World War II and how banks for many years had "red-lined" African Americans from purchasing homes in desired neighborhoods throughout major metropolitan areas, but she had never heard about buying houses on contract. It made sense though; blocked from formal borrowing opportunities, African Americans were pushed into a secondary loan market that preyed on their vulnerability and lack of experience. It was yet another way in which African Americans had been kept from the benefits of homeownership and securing a piece of "the American dream."

It made her furious to think about it.

Mrs. Johnson continued. "After that experience, my parents drilled it into our heads that we should do everything by the book, with a well-known bank. So me and Mr. Johnson, we saved our down payment. And we paid that loan off in thirty years, to the day.

"That must have been a good feeling," said Martha, with a big smile.

"Oh, it was, honey, don't you know it!" replied Mrs. Johnson.

Martha felt a twinge of uncertainty. So far, the story sounded like the Johnsons had been able to avoid the pitfalls of homeownership.

"That was in 1995," Mrs. Johnson continued. "But a few years later, we started getting calls from a mortgage company. The man on the phone said they had refinanced the loan for the church we go to and that we could use our home to get a low-interest loan."

"I'm confused," interrupted Jessie. "I thought you said you had paid off your loans?"

"That's right, we did," answered Mrs. Johnson. "But if you own your home, the bank will loan you money because they know you can always sell your house to pay them back."

"In other words," interjected Martha, "to banks, people like the Johnsons are a good risk."

"Oh," said Jessie, "I get it."

Mrs. Johnson continued with the story. "Well, at first we didn't pay him no heed, but then we heard about how much tuition our grandkids were having to pay, and we thought we could help them out. So we took out a $45,000 loan. But it wasn't like the previous loans we were used to."

"What do you mean?" asked Martha.

"Well, when we bought our house we made payments to the same bank for thirty years. But with this one, within a week we received a letter saying the bank had sold our loan to some other bank. And that bank sold it to a different bank. Seems like every time I looked around we were writing a check to a different bank!"

Martha was trying to figure out why banks would sell loans to other banks, but she needed to keep up with Mrs. Johnson's explanation.

"The other reason it was different is that we paid the same interest rate on our previous loans, but this one kept going up and up."

It sounded to Martha like the Johnsons had been given an adjustable rate mortgage, often referred to as an ARM, which she knew was a popular tactic used by banks and mortgage companies over the past few years.

"At first, everything was okay, we made the higher payments, but after Mr. Johnson's eyes went bad, he couldn't work anymore. We got the loan modified, but that just added a bunch of fees, and the payments just kept getting higher and higher."

Martha started to get a sick feeling in her stomach and feared that she knew where the story was headed. From the other room she heard the announcer say that it was the top of the ninth inning.

"Now, let me say this," Mrs. Johnson continued as her eyes began to moisten. "We cannot sell this house. My daughter wants to get married in the backyard, and Mr. Johnson can get around because he knows every foot of this place. These aren't just four walls, this is a refuge, this is where our children grew up. And it's where we want to end our days."

Martha looked at Jessie, who was sitting on the edge of the sofa, totally engrossed in what Mrs. Johnson was saying.

Mrs. Johnson soldiered on. "You know, I wanted to leave this house for our children, but now it's worth less than our loan, and we haven't been able to make payments in months. The bank says we need to be out by next month, and I just don't know what to do."

Martha knew that there were no easy answers to the tragedy that Mr. and Mrs. Johnson were experiencing and that listening was the best thing she could offer in the moment. But a burning question needed to be asked.

"Mrs. Johnson," Martha politely inquired, "if you don't mind me asking, how much do you still owe on that original $45,000 loan?"

Pushed to an emotional limit, the elderly woman somehow managed to keep her composure. She looked directly in Martha's eyes and said "$190,000."

MARTHA WAS INCENSED at the injustice and trauma that the Johnsons were experiencing. Though she was well aware of the prejudicial ways in which housing markets had traditionally excluded African Americans, the predatory exploitation that Mrs. Johnson had recounted was beyond anything she had heard. She resolved to help the Johnsons in any way she could, but first she had to educate herself about trends in housing and mortgage industry practices. A good place to start would be to sit down with Florence Bossier, one of her board members. She remembered talking briefly with Florence before a board meeting about her volunteer work as a housing advocate with the National Association for the Advancement of Colored People. She hoped that Florence would have some ideas about how the Johnsons could restructure their loan or perhaps receive some financial assistance to defray foreclosure.

A meeting Martha arranged with Florence the next week was instructive. She learned that, as a result of the housing boom, the mortgage market had essentially tapped out the number of White households it could effectively market for homeownership and had thus turned its gaze to African Americans, the very population it had for so many years mistreated. She learned that during the New Deal Blacks had not been allowed to benefit from housing programs like the Home Owners Loan Corporation, and after World War II Black veterans had essentially been denied low-interest loans as part of the GI Bill. She learned about violent riots that took place in the 1940s and 1950s in Chicago wherein White gangs attacked and beat Black families living in "white" sections of the city. Martha couldn't help but think that, even though she was a child when these events happened, Mrs. Johnson would no doubt remember them and the fear they instilled. Finally, she learned that recent studies had shown that Black homebuyers were being given subprime mortgages—mortgages that came with unfavorable terms, like those given to the Johnsons, even when their credit histories were good. According to the research Florence had conducted, a significant percentage of subprime borrowers were facing default and foreclosure on their home loans.

To Martha, the historical scope of the discrimination and the details of its current incarnation were beyond imagination. It was clear that throughout US history, African Americans had been preyed upon in the housing industry, first through exclusion and then through blatant exploitation that took many forms. The Johnsons were pawns in an injustice whose roots stretched deep into the past, and Martha knew there would be no easy fix to the financial hole they were in. Thankfully, Florence had gone the extra mile and secured the pro bono assistance of a real estate attorney. The attorney let Florence know that the Johnsons had been given a *negative amortization* mortgage coupled with an adjustable rate. This type of mortgage is designed to reduce payments early in the loan period; in the Johnson's case, payments they had made were less than the interest due, and the difference had been added to the loan balance year after year. The only good news was that the attorney had been able to negotiate a few more months before the Johnsons would face foreclosure and eviction.

During the summer months, the newspaper headlines increasingly reported bleak economic statistics. Responding to the economic downturn and corporations posting record losses, the Bush administration passed a $110 billion tax rebate to stimulate the economy, but in July consumer spending began to plummet and unemployment rates continued to increase. The downturn could be seen in the numbers that were showing up at Helping Hands for assistance. Martha had read that job losses were particularly hurting young workers, those under thirty, and saw evidence of this among the people waiting in line for assistance, which often wrapped around the building.

September 2008

In September, the whole financial world seemed to fall apart. Newspaper headlines proclaimed bank failures and various emergency efforts on the part

of the Federal Reserve and the US Treasury to save a rapidly deteriorating banking system. On September 7 the headlines noted that the federal government had taken over mortgage giants Fannie Mae and Freddie Mac; on September 15 Bank of America purchased Merrill Lynch, and Lehman Brothers, a 150-year-old investment bank with over 26,000 employees, filed for bankruptcy. Martha was already upset about the effects of the housing crisis on her neighbor, but her understanding of the global roots of the causes was limited. Finding herself near the campus, she decided to stop by Professor Gault's office. She knew her former policy professor could provide a more complete picture. Martha tapped at his partially opened door and found him engrossed in a news report on his computer. He was practically yelling at the screen when she entered the room.

"Hi, Martha!" Dr. Gault exclaimed. "I've been following the BBC online about the financial crash, and I have to say, I'm as angry as I've ever been in my life!"

"I hear you about being angry," Martha replied. "My elderly neighbor is facing foreclosure after taking out a mortgage to help her grandchildren pay for college. Yet an op-ed I read the other day blamed the crisis on shifty homeowners using their homes as ATMs."

"It's much more than people taking out loans they couldn't afford, Martha," Dr. Gault began. "This whole crisis was bound to happen, and the entire financial system is at fault, from the mortgage companies, to the banks, to credit rating agencies and the government. I'm really tired of the media blaming the victims again. How about we head over to the student union and talk over lunch?"

Over the next hour, Dr. Gault explained the roots of the housing crisis and its connection to the overall financial system. Martha's head was filled with terms such as "collateralized debt obligations," "securitization food chains," and "credit default swaps"—terms created as a result of complex financial products and services designed after Congress repealed the Glass-Steagall Act that had been passed during the Great Depression. Glass-Steagall kept investment banks separate from banks that gave out home, car, and other personal loans to the public. As Dr. Gault noted, it took only a few years after the repeal of Glass-Steagall for the entire world financial system to spiral out of control.

"It's really all about deregulation and greed, Martha," Dr. Gault said. "Wall Street decided to gamble with retirement plans, home loans, student loans, and other loans, using them as a security product, just like a mutual fund. The way in which homeowners were drawn in is particularly disgusting, in my opinion. Do you remember President Bush talking about the 'ownership society,' saying every American ought to realize the dream of owning a home?"

"Yes, of course," Martha replied. "I remember thinking that the higher home ownership rates were one of the few things that the Bush administration could justifiably crow about. But based on my neighbor's experience, it now feels to me as though people were set up to fail."

"That's exactly right, Martha. They *were* set up." In an explanation that mirrored her conversations with Florence, Dr. Gault described how the housing market had essentially "dried up." Using the traditional criteria for giving loans, most of the wealthy and middle class that were able had already purchased homes, leaving a shrinking market of potential homebuyers in the United States. If the banks wanted to package mortgages and other debt as a security to sell to investors, they needed an influx of homebuyers.

"So," Dr. Gault continued, "they deliberately targeted working-class families and elderly people, offering them 'low-interest loans' with ballooning interest and hidden fees, making the paperwork so complicated that few really understood what they were getting into. And once they had these loans in place, they simply packaged them with other debts and sold them to investors who thought they could make money off the interest from the loans." Dr. Gault waited for Martha to digest what she had just heard.

"If I understand this correctly then," Martha began, "the bank had no incentive at all to be sure that people could afford the payments or would know what the payments would look like after a few years.

"That's right," said Dr. Gault. "In the worst cases, the mortgage companies didn't even care if homebuyers could pay back loans because they were just going to sell them off anyway."

"That's just crazy!" Martha exclaimed incredulously.

"Yes, and to make matters even worse, insurance companies like AIG sold insurance on those investments, not just to the investor holding the loan but to *anyone*," Dr. Gault replied.

"Wait a minute," Martha said. "Are you saying that if my home loan were part of those deals, some stranger who doesn't know me at all could buy insurance against my paying the loan? Wouldn't that mean if I couldn't pay my debt, there might be multiple people who could collect on the policy?" Martha was even more incredulous.

"That's precisely what I'm saying, Martha. It's why AIG and Lehman Brothers are all over the news right now. Lehman went bankrupt and shut down the financial business of millions of people around the world. AIG didn't keep enough money in their coffers to actually cover all the plans they sold, so they now owe more than they can pay. And Treasury Secretary Paulson, a former Goldman Sachs CEO, wants taxpayers to bail out the financial institutions that started this whole racket!"

Martha sat at the table experiencing a vast range of emotions. She thought of all the people who were being evicted across the country due to the greed and duplicitous behavior of Wall Street bankers. She was particularly upset about the Johnsons' plight and saw in their experience the intersection of historical discrimination, a banking system let loose to prey on hard-working Americans, and a political system that turned a blind eye to the whole thing. How were people like the Johnsons supposed to understand what was happening if the whole system was just a big swindle? The idea of bailing out financial companies that played an integral role in the crisis made her furious. She asked Dr. Gault if the government was going to do anything to help homeowners who were duped as part of the scheme.

"I certainly hope so, Martha, but I have my doubts," he said. "The role of Congress in this is clear. Their desire to deregulate financial markets and allow the bankers to run roughshod over us has driven policy since the Reagan administration. And Clinton was really no better; obviously, Glass-Steagall was repealed on his watch. The Bush administration added humongous tax breaks for the wealthy on top of this, but the process was already underway when he took office."

"I read today that McCain is suspending his campaign to work on the crisis," Martha replied. "Do you think that's going to accomplish much?"

"I doubt it," Dr. Gault replied quickly. "McCain hasn't shown much leadership on these issues in the past, and his choice of Sarah Palin as a running mate isn't inspiring much confidence, even among members of his own party. And Obama is a junior member of the Senate, so it's doubtful that he will be allowed to exercise leadership. It's just a mess right now. But I'm sure we'll hear something from them in the upcoming debate. The only thing I know for sure is that, at this point, doing nothing is not an option."

Martha took a moment to digest this information. "I also read that we're all going to be affected by this, even if we didn't take out a loan," said Martha.

"True enough," said Dr. Gault, "because the rating agencies were paid by the investment banks to give the best rating, an AAA, to these debt obligations, our retirement plans also invested in them. Have you taken a look at your latest statement, Martha?"

"Allen and I were just talking about the hit our plans took the other day," she said. "If we were closer to retirement age, there would be no way we could stop working. And what about retirees who rely on investments for their income? What is happening to them?"

"They are just going to suffer," Dr. Gault said. "There's no two ways about it. All I can say is 'thank God for Social Security,' as that's the only safe investment out there right now. Whenever we hear a politician talk about privatizing Social Security again, I hope we remember this fiasco."

Martha drove back to Helping Hands after her conversation with Dr. Gault and walked into the lobby to see Julia speaking with Stan, the grumpy part-time accountant who helped keep the books. Julia cut the conversation off mid-sentence and Stan was smiling, so Martha knew something was up.

"OK, what's going on?" Martha inquired.

"Just a minute," Julia replied, giggling like a teenager who couldn't keep a secret. She made a quick call and soon Ruth and Melissa entered the lobby.

"Que pasa, pues?" asked Ruth. At least, Martha thought, I'm not the only one in the dark.

"Go ahead," Julia said to Stan. "Tell 'em!"

"Well," said Stan, clearing his throat, "when I looked at the bank account today, I noticed a very large sum of money had been wired into our account last night. At first I didn't know where it was from, but I think it represents the first year of funding for the ACF (Administration for Children and Families) grant we submitted."

A moment of silence ensued as the five Helping Hands staff members looked at each other in disbelief.

"Are you kidding me!?" Martha gasped.

"You know me, Martha, I'm a pretty serious guy," Stan replied, just before a big smile crossed his face.

Melissa, who was now going to be hired full-time to work on the interprofessional family education project, gave Ruth a big hug and was quickly joined by Julia and Martha.

"I can't believe this," Martha stated incredulously. "I've never heard of a grant being announced this way."

A few days later, an acceptance letter from the AFC arrived in the mail. For the next three years, Helping Hands would partner with two nursing programs, the local School of Social Work, and the Department of Health Services to improve postnatal child and family outcomes among young parents in River City through a novel home-visiting program.

October 2008

October arrived with a bang. The newspapers were filled with stories from pundits discussing the impact of the first presidential debate between Barack

THE PRESIDENTIAL ELECTION OF 2008...

Obama and John McCain and the vice-presidential debate between Senator Joe Biden and Alaska governor Sarah Palin—the first debate to feature a female candidate since Geraldine Ferraro in 1984. The business news was dominated by passage of the $700 billion Troubled Asset Relief Program (TARP). Though Congress had voted down previous versions, TARP was passed in both houses and signed into law by President Bush. Unfortunately, Dr. Gault's skeptical prognostication proved correct. Within days, it became clear that rather than pushing homeowner relief, TARP was going to be a massive bailout for the large financial institutions that had created the mess in the first place. Martha read reports in the news stating that the banks were simply too big to fail; other more critical voices noted the negative implications of the incestuous relationships between Wall Street and members of the Treasury and Federal Reserve. Over $100 billion dollars were given to nine major banks, with little administrative oversight and only a few token restrictions on how the money could be spent. Martha shook her head in frustration; the paperwork required for a hungry family to apply for and receive food stamps was more extensive than what was required for a bank to receive billions in tax dollars.

Martha watched all three of the debates between Obama and McCain and even accepted an invitation from Dr. Gault to watch an alternative party debate among other presidential candidates who had not been allowed in the "official" debates. The man she had voted for in the 2000 presidential election, Ralph Nader, impressed her with his knowledge of statistics and policy, and she was also impressed with Green Party nominee Cynthia McKinney, an African American woman and former six-time Congressional Representative from Georgia.

November 2008

On November 4, Martha invited a few of her stalwart political friends to watch the election night coverage. The excitement continued to build as Martha switched back and forth between several stations over the course of the evening, but a few hours after the polls closed it became clear that Barack Obama was going to become the next president of the United States. At around 11 p.m. eastern time, the newscasters on MSNBC made it official. Barack Obama had garnered 60 million votes and some 360 electoral votes, well over the 270 votes needed to win the office. Martha hugged Allen and began to cry when she heard the newsman from ABC state that Barack Obama had overcome a barrier as old as the Republic itself. Though a few of her friends left, Martha and Allen remained glued to the television coverage of Obama's acceptance speech from Grant Park in Chicago, where nearly a quarter of a million people gathered to celebrate the election of the first African American president in US history. She listened intently to his words when he said:

> If there is anyone out there who still doubts that America is a place where all things are possible, who still wonders if the dream of our founders is alive in our time, who still questions the power of our democracy, tonight is your answer.

Martha hoped his words were true.

Acknowledgments

The example of Mr. and Mrs. Johnson in this chapter was taken directly from a case study in *A Dream Foreclosed* (Gottesdiener, 2013).

Discussion Questions

1. Stigma is usually an important reason why otherwise eligible households do not apply for public welfare benefits, like food stamps, to which they are entitled. Discuss ways in which stigma associated with safety net programs could be reduced.

2. In 1988, President Reagan signed legislation that offered a formal apology and $20,000 to every person of Japanese ancestry that had been forcibly relocated and interred in camps during World War II. In the wake of this precedent, numerous calls have been made for the US government to offer reparations to African Americans on the basis of centuries of forced servitude and discriminatory policies. Discuss the strengths and limits of this potential policy.

3. Investigate how funds for the TARP were spent. What financial institutions and corporations received the largest bailouts? How much money has been paid back? How large was the overall bailout compared to other components of the federal budget (e.g., SNAP)? One of the conditions for receiving TARP funds included limits on executive pay. Do you agree with this? Why or why not?

4. The sheer size of the bailout is hard to comprehend and actually includes much more money than was included in the TARP. This is a fun exercise to get a handle on the scope of the government (read: taxpayer) largesse. One day Bill Gates was feeling particularly generous and decided to give out $1 million, one dollar every second. How long would it take him to distribute the money? (Answer: about 11 days). Not wanting to be outdone, Warren Buffet decides to hand out $1 billion, one dollar every second. How long would it take to hand out the money?

Suggested Readings

Anderson, Devery. (2015). *Emmitt Till: The murder that shocked the world and propelled the civil rights movement.* Jackson: University Press of Mississippi.

Ayres, William. (1998). *A kind and just parent.* Boston: Beacon Press.

Burtless, Gary. (2009, December). The "Great Recession" and redistribution: Federal antipoverty policies. Institute for Research on Poverty. *Fast Focus*.

Coates, Ta-Nehisi (2014, June). The case for reparations. *The Atlantic*. Retrieved from http://www.theatlantic.com/magazine/archive/2014/06/the-case-for-reparations/361631/

Dayen, David. (2015, Winter). A needless default. *The American Prospect*.

Delaney, Arthur. (2013, August 15). Food stamps avoided by millions of eligible Americans. *Huffington Post*. Retrieved from http://www.huffingtonpost.com/2013/08/14/food-stamps_n_3757052.html

Eichengreen, Barry. (2015). *Hall of mirrors: The Great Depression, the Great Recession, and the uses—and misuses—of history*. New York: Oxford University Press.

Food Research and Action Center. (n.d.). SNAP/food stamps participation data. Retrieved from http://frac.org/reports-and-resources/snapfood-stamp-monthly-participation-data/

Gottesdiener, Laura. (2013). *A dream foreclosed: Black America and the fight for a place to call home*. Hull, MA: Zucotti Park Press.

Kroll, Andy. (2009, May 26). The greatest swindle ever sold. *The Nation*.

Senate Agriculture, Nutrition, and Forestry Committee. (n.d.) Farm bill: Investments for the future. Retrieved from http://www.agriculture.senate.gov/imo/media/doc/2008_farm_bill_highlights.pdf

Wilkerson, Isabel. (2011). *The warmth of other suns: The epic story of America's Great Migration*. New York: Vintage.

5

Great Recession Realities

November 2008

While Melissa was absolutely thrilled with the election of Barack Obama, she also believed that the country had taken a huge step backwards. A ballot initiative to stop gay marriage in California was passed after a significant effort by religious groups. No more same-sex marriage licenses would be issued in California. As far as Melissa could tell, she and Kris and about 18,000 other same-sex couples who had married since June would still have their marriages recognized until court battles over this new law were completed. However, Melissa found the tenacity with which the religious and anti-gay forces had funded and attacked equal rights to be shocking. It was clear that the election of an African American man to the highest office in the land did not signal a sea change for LGBTQ rights in the United States.

Melissa and Martha went to dinner after work a few days after the election. Martha knew how upset Melissa was and offered her encouragement and hope for the future. "You know, Melissa, my children have been raised in a time when the idea of gay couples is a norm for them. They have friends who came out in high school, and for them it was no big deal. On the other hand, I had a friend in high school who left River City and moved to California just to get away from the prejudice he faced. The acceptance just wasn't there a generation ago, but today, you have allies who want to fight with you."

"I know it's a different world now, Martha. I do feel that we're making progress. At the same time, I don't understand how so many people can be so vehemently opposed to loving adults having the right to be married. How does it hurt anyone? How does it 'lessen the value of heterosexual marriage'?"

Martha shook her head, and Melissa's eyes filled with tears. "Kris and I love each other and are committed regardless of what others may think.

I wish I didn't care if others disapproved; perhaps if they didn't control my access to the same privileges they enjoy, I could just ignore them." They spent the rest of dinner discussing the many ways in which pro-marriage equality groups could fight back.

Martha went home after dinner and had a long talk with Allen about Melissa's situation. "Honey, do you realize how lucky we are? I mean, we know what discrimination feels like, but at least our relationship is recognized and we have all the benefits that come with a legal marriage. I just hate what is happening to Melissa right now."

Allen replied that he was certain the momentum was on Melissa's side and one day gay marriage would be legal. "I don't know when it will happen, but our kids will be the leaders of this country one day. Young people just don't have the same issues that we grew up with. I remember a couple of kids back when I was in elementary school were always getting taunted. They just don't let that kind of stuff happen anymore."

Though Martha wasn't as confident as Allen about the extent of change that had taken place, she appreciated what he had to say. And she hoped that President-elect Obama, as an African American, would follow Martin Luther King's famous dictum: "Injustice anywhere is a threat to justice everywhere." She hoped that Obama would use the power of government to combat discrimination and promote equal treatment.

As Martha entered the office early one morning two weeks after the election, she was filled with anticipation about the future. In the last year the US and world economy had been in free fall, and Helping Hands had lost their primary source of funding while struggling to meet the needs of a growing number of hungry families and unemployed workers. But for the first time in history, an African American had been elected president of the United States. Martha had only dreamed that something like this would happen in her lifetime. She had a renewed sense of hope when she thought about what the election meant for the future. After 200 years of having only Caucasian men as presidents, a new era had arrived, and American voters had affirmed that an African American could indeed achieve the highest political office in the land. Martha had seen the worst of what the economic crisis was doing to everyday Americans, and she hoped that President Obama would immediately push for bold policy efforts. The first 100 days of a presidency were thought to define the agenda and perhaps even establish the legacy of a president. Martha knew that the new president would have his hands full after inheriting a monumental economic crisis and two foreign wars of occupation. There would be no honeymoon for President-elect Obama and plenty who would oppose his leadership and cheer any missteps he might make.

Turning on the lights in her office, Martha was immediately thrust back into her day-to-day reality. This was going to be an important week for the new program. Its name, the Early Intervention Home Visiting Program, said it all. It was based on a model from an evidence-based program overseas. Martha had perused the Administration for Children and Families (ACF) website for models that had significant research behind their effectiveness and had been deemed "evidence-based" by the federal government. While this model utilized nurses only, Helping Hands adapted the program to include social workers, a focus on interprofessional education, and mentoring. The goal of the program was to bring different skill sets and knowledge bases together to work with new parents, specifically mothers deemed at risk due to lack of support, alcohol, and/or drug abuse, previous history of mental health treatment, or other life stressors such as domestic violence. The new program added a measure of financial stability to Helping Hands, and, at least for the next few years, Martha did not have to worry about losing valuable employees for lack of funds.

Martha had a consultant coming for a week to begin training the staff in the Family Partnership Model, including two nurses and a brand-new social worker in addition to Melissa and Ruth. This model was evidence-based and had more than twenty years of research to support its efficacy. She liked this model in particular, as it was used extensively over the years in the UK and Australia, had a strengths-based orientation, and utilized many of the values and skills in which the profession of social work was particularly well grounded.

Martha listened to her voicemail and then made her way to the conference room where the training would take place. Melissa and Ruth were already at work setting up, with packets of training materials in front of each seat. They had received the information from Terry Webster, the consultant from the Centre for Parent and Child Support in England. Fortunately for Martha, Robert, one of her board members, had contributed frequent flyer miles to cover Terry's travel, saving the grant from this expense and allowing Martha to show the ACF that they had community support for the program.

"There's the dynamic duo, already hard at work!" Martha exclaimed with a big smile. With years of experience as a public school teacher and as the primary trainer for the successful welfare-to-work program that Helping Hands had run for years, Ruth was slated to be the lead trainer in the Family Partnership Model. She had also written a bilingual curriculum that was designed to help parents understand their child's development and to communicate effectively with teachers, social workers, nurses, and others who might be involved in their lives through the program.

"I'm so excited about this next phase, Martha!" Ruth exclaimed. "We're branching out in ways that I never expected." Even though they had served young parents for years by providing clothing and food, emergency rent, utilities, transportation, skills training, and childcare, this was the first time Helping Hands was formally working in the arena of child welfare.

"The partnerships we've created over the years certainly helped us get this grant," Martha replied. "I know it was helpful that I have child welfare experience, but I am convinced the collaboration with the university and the community college made our proposal stand out."

"I agree," interjected Melissa while placing the last of the materials on the table. "I took elective courses outside of social work as part of my degree, but I think it would have been better if they had been taught in an interdisciplinary way."

"Pues, mejor tarde que nunca," replied Ruth in her customary way of using short Spanish phrases with co-workers.

"That means better late than never, right?" asked Melissa as Ruth grinned and nodded affirmatively.

As they were finishing up, Julia arrived with Terry Webster, the consultant, and introduced her to the Helping Hands staff. Terry expressed her delight in finally meeting Martha and for the opportunity to see the Family Partnership Model used, as she lightheartedly put it, "across the pond."

"Our program has been in operation for years, but it's only recently that your government cited us as an 'evidenced-based' program," Terry said. "The interest in what we do has been quite exciting, but this is our first time actually coming to the United States to help start a new program."

"Well, I hope you're not too jet-lagged to do the training!" Martha laughed. "I know when I traveled to Oxford a few years ago, it took me a few days to recover."

Terry grinned at Martha and Ruth. "Nothing that a few good nursing tricks and some strong Earl Grey can't nip in the bud! I can't tell you how excited I am to be here to help you get started."

The rest of the staff arrived shortly thereafter, as did Dr. Gault and Dr. Marie Montiel from the university's nursing program. They were attending the training for the purposes of their own curriculum development for the interprofessional education program in social work and nursing. Melissa, Ruth, Hayley, an undergraduate social work intern, and Emma, the recently hired social worker, were excitedly chatting away, as were the newly hired nurses, John and Katie, who had bonded quickly with the social workers. The conference room was full of both people and enthusiasm, and for the next few days everyone immersed themselves in the theory and practice behind the Family Partnership Model.

At home a few weeks later, with the program on the verge of accepting its first referrals, Martha received a call from Florence Bossier, one of her advisory board members. "I've got some bad news, Martha. The bank plans to evict the Johnsons in a few days and put their house up for auction."

Martha had been so busy getting the new program up and running that she had forgotten the Johnsons were reaching the end of the extra time the attorney had negotiated for them. Luckily, Florence had kept up with the issue. "Is there anything else that can be done?" Martha asked.

Florence answered with her customary zeal. "Well, there is, Martha, but it's not for the faint of heart. We need to disrupt both the eviction and the auction because it's clear the bank isn't about to give in."

"I was afraid there would be no easy solution," Martha replied with an air of resignation.

"You're right, Martha, there isn't," Florence replied in a matter-of-fact tone. "So the question I have for you, is, are you in? And I think you know what I mean when I ask, because this situation can't be handled with half-measures."

Martha knew what she meant, and she knew what being evicted would do to the Johnsons. She thought about her former neighbors who had been forced to leave, about the lines of needy people that snaked around Helping Hands, about banks that were too big to fail while families were being pushed into the winter cold.

"Count me in," she said.

The following week at 6:30 AM Martha stamped her feet to keep warm as she stood on the Johnson's porch. She and Florence had hatched a plan, a two-pronged attack of sorts, to disrupt both the eviction and the auction. Martha's role was to organize the neighbors and other volunteers to impede the eviction while Florence attended the auction. Martha surveyed the quiet neighborhood, shivering, and for a moment wondered if her discussions with neighbors and the flyers she had posted had done any good.

And then they came.

Just a few at first, neighbors in thick winter coats with wool hats and scarves that could not hide the determination on their faces. Joined by the Johnsons' children and grandchildren and their friends, by 7:30 a ring of

WAITING TO GET SUPPLIES FROM THE FOOD PANTRY...

© SHARON RUDAHL 2015

people stood around the house. At 7:45 two neighbors parked their cars across the road to block access to that section of the neighborhood. At 8:00 one of the neighbors, a Katrina evacuee who had been denied access to his ninth ward home in New Orleans for months after the storm, showed up with a barbeque. "Oh hell y'all," he shouted to cheers as he set up the grill, "if we gonna do this, then we gonna do it right!"

At 9:00 the sheriff came.

Across town, just as the auction was to begin, Florence, Rev. Anderson, and a handful of his congregation slipped into the room. A reporter and a photographer from the *River City Star* followed them. When the Johnson's house came up for bid, the auctioneer started at $12,000. Florence raised her hand.

"I have twelve thousand," said the auctioneer, "do I hear eighteen thousand?" At that moment, Rev. Anderson began to clap and lead his congregants in a particularly spirited version of *This Little Heart of Mine*. It was too loud for the auctioneer to continue. Though confused at first, the bank representatives became angry and threatened to have the singers thrown out of the building. Upon hearing this, members of Rev. Anderson's congregation sitting among the assembled crowd joined in the singing and clapping. With the cacophony in full roar, Florence took aside one of the bank representatives and pointed out the reporters.

"Do you really want this to be on the front page of tomorrow's paper?" she asked. The frowning representative disappeared into a back room. Twenty minutes and many verses later, he reappeared. Leaning into Florence's ear, he shouted, "Okay, the house has been sold for $12,000." Florence smiled and gave a thumbs up to the assembled crowd. The tumult of celebration in the room was deafening.

"Hallelujah!" Rev. Anderson exclaimed as he led the singers around the room and down the halls on their way out of the building.

Across town, Martha was receiving congratulations from her neighbors.

"I can't believe you faced down the sheriff!" one of them exclaimed.

"I just held my ground," said Martha, looking at all the neighbors and volunteers who had gathered around the house. "We all just held our ground!"

"You did more than that!" a voice behind her exclaimed. She turned around to see Mr. Johnson emerging through the front door holding Mrs. Johnson's arm. "You used soul force, and it doesn't get any stronger than that!" He reached out to Martha and gave her a big hug while everyone cheered.

January 2009

Knowing how difficult it could be to receive an adequate number of referrals, Martha was relieved that local hospitals, as well as the Department of Human Services, were sending referrals to the new program. Melissa, Martha's choice to coordinate the new program, sorted through them with the staff. Each week, a team meeting was held to review and assign new cases to staff, complete an in-depth case conference on a selected client, and provide support and consultation to one another. Martha was pleased with the way the staff worked together; they got along well and respected the model of collaboration between social work and nursing. Martha had reached out to the career services offices in nursing and social work and informed them about jobs and internships that would be part of the new program, which increased the number of applications from well-qualified applicants. Each person hired had experience in the field and had already worked in a team setting with other disciplines. They had come prepared and were excited to be a part of this program. It was the first of its kind in River City; and with the support of the Council of Community Services and the notoriety Martha had gained leading the investigation of the financial practices of the Children's Corner, Helping Hands had already received positive attention in the media. A feature story on the Early Intervention Home Visiting Program had run in the paper, and a local television news station had interviewed Martha and Carlene about their efforts to start the program.

As Martha neared the lunchroom she could hear a serious conversation taking place. "I hope Obama does a massive jobs program, just like Roosevelt did during the New Deal," Melissa was saying as Martha walked in. Ruth, Melissa, and a new nursing student, Daniel, were eating lunch. With the inauguration just days away, they were discussing what they thought Obama should do first.

Daniel, who had served two tours of duty in Iraq in the Army before returning to college to major in nursing, had a very different idea about Obama's first policy moves.

"I think he should focus on veteran's services, especially for all those who served in Iraq and Afghanistan," he shared. "I know it sounds self-serving, but no one serving now is doing so without making a conscious decision to join the military and serve their country. You always know you might be sent into a war zone, but men and women still sign up anyway." Daniel was clearly alarmed by the high rates of suicide among returning vets and related his difficult experiences trying to procure appropriate mental health care for a buddy who had served with him.

"But Daniel, don't you think many people join due to the lack of jobs available?" Melissa asked. "I believe veterans should be supported and cared for, but if we had a jobs program the military wouldn't be viewed as the only option for so many. Only about a quarter of adults in the United States get a four-year degree, so there's a great need to fill the gap in jobs that are disappearing."

"That's not why I joined," replied Daniel. "I just wasn't ready for college and I wanted to serve my country."

"I'm sorry," apologized Melissa. "I wasn't referring to you, personally."

"I know," said Daniel, smiling. "Don't worry, we're good."

Martha thought a slight adjustment might help the conversation. "Well, to go back to the theme of health care, we live in a state with a high number of uninsured people. I hope he tackles the health care situation. Personally, I wish we'd just have 'Medicare for all' or some type of national health insurance program. Did you see the film *Sicko*? The parts about the French and English systems were unbelievable."

"To be honest, I haven't seen the movie," Daniel quickly replied. "But from what I know of the way the VA runs, I don't think you want the government running health care." Daniel was referring to a series of scandals that had recently rocked the VA about fabricated patient wait times and atrocious conditions at VA facilities.

"Well, what's Obama supposed to do?" countered Ruth. "Here we are on the front lines and we can't agree on what should be a priority."

A thoughtful silence filled the air after Ruth's query.

"You're right, Ruth," said Melissa. "So here's what I think. Obama should focus on the one issue everyone can agree on."

"And what would that be?" asked Ruth with more than a hint of skepticism.

"Well, the way I see it, everyone is really upset with the big banks right now. They were buying and selling bad debt, like house and car loans, and student loans in big bundles, and then betting they might default. They bought insurance to cover themselves in case that happened, and now AIG is in big trouble."

"So what do you think Obama should do?" asked Martha, intrigued with the direction the conversation was going.

"I think the US government, that is, the taxpayers, should have an ownership stake in all these banks and corporations we're bailing out with TARP money," she replied with no hesitation. *The New York Times* had recently run some stories to the effect that hundreds of billions of dollars had immediately run through the Troubled Asset Relief Program straight to a handful of the largest banks, with few provisions or conditions attached. "And it doesn't make any sense that taxpayers are bailing out the banks and not the people that the banks scammed."

"Wait a minute, Melissa," Daniel replied. "I don't think anyone forced all those homeowners to take out those loans. I read something that said people were just jumping on the bandwagon during the boom but when it came time to pay up they couldn't."

Martha quickly thought about the Johnsons' situation but stanched the urge to immediately respond. "That's certainly the standard line," Melissa replied. "But my partner and I just purchased a home and the terms were really confusing. And a couple of weeks after we bought the house the mortgage was sold to some other company," she added. "We have college degrees and we were confused. I can only imagine how confusing it must be to someone with limited English fluency, to use just one example." Daniel didn't respond but nodded his head to indicate that he was listening. Martha was impressed with his ability to listen to a differing opinion. Listening was often referred to as a "soft skill," but Martha knew it was an aptitude that took patience and intention. It was hard to teach but one that is critical to successful practice in the helping professions like nursing and social work.

Three days later, Martha gathered the available staff in the lunchroom to watch an inaugural celebration for Obama at the Lincoln Memorial. The announcers stated that some 400,000 people were on hand to watch the historic event. Martha made a mental note to keep it together in front of her staff, but she was surprised how emotional she became when Bruce Springsteen and Pete Seeger, supporters of Obama's candidacy from early in his campaign, led off the festivities with a rousing rendition of Woody Guthrie's Great Depression classic "This Land Is Your Land." Martha closed her eyes and listened to the verses that are usually ignored in the public school renditions she had heard:

> In the square of the city-In the shadow of the steeple
> In the relief office-I saw my people
> As they stood there hungry—I stood there whistling
> This land was still made for you and me.
>
> A great high wall there that tried to stop me;
> A great big sign there said private property;
> But on the other side it didn't say nothing;
> That side was made for you and me.

Martha knew that many African Americans viewed Obama's election as a personal victory, a vindication of sorts in the long march to freedom. She couldn't help but feel the hope that Obama had so eloquently articulated in many of his campaign speeches. Over 90% of African American voters had cast their ballots for Obama, and a historic outpouring of support from young voters had helped turn the tide his way. She also knew that Obama's victory represented the pinnacle accomplishment of Black activists over the years, who felt that more could be gained from winning over presidents and governors than attempting to sway large political bodies like Congress or state legislatures. But Martha's joy was tempered by the day-to-day realities she faced at Helping Hands. In River City and across the country the recession was decimating Black households; unemployment rates among African American males were sky high, and policies promoting mass incarceration continued to have a disproportionate impact on African Americans. She wondered if having a Black president would make it more difficult for Black leaders to speak out against injustice, or if Obama himself would hedge his views with regard to the problems faced by African Americans in an attempt to avoid the appearance of racial favoritism. This, she knew, was a problem that Caucasian presidents never had to consider.

Martha had read a breakdown of the recent election and saw cause for hope and concern. Obama had won by an electoral landslide: 365 votes to McCain's 173. The Republicans had lost 57 seats in the House and seven seats in the Senate. Obama had dominated the youth vote through his innovative use of the Internet and social media, and Martha had read opinions suggesting that the Millennial generation was finally putting an end to electoral racism. Yet McCain, who despite his "maverick" status and woeful selection of Sarah Palin as a running mate, had still won almost half of the states, 15 of them by double digits. And it was the norm for voters to switch parties after a single-party presidential term of eight years. So, was this a significant shift to the left or just voter frustration with the economy and politics as usual?

As she watched the jubilant celebration, Martha couldn't help but think about the question that Martin Luther King had so poignantly asked many years previously: "Where do we go from here?"

February 2009

As part of the new interprofessional education program at the university, Martha, Melissa, and Katie were asked to guest speak in the interdisciplinary course being taught by Dr. Gault and Dr. Montiel. The two were team-teaching social work and nursing students in a new course, titled Interprofessional Practice with Families and Children. Though it was early in the grant's implementation, Martha's staff had been invited to share their perspectives on the program model they were using as part of their grant.

"We're fortunate to have graduates from our two programs working in one of our community's first ever interprofessional practice efforts," began Dr. Montiel. "We know that nurses and social workers often collaborate on cases in health care systems. We also know that there has been some friction between the two professions over the issue of case management in hospital settings. Our program at the university is attempting to remove such competition and integrate best practices from both professions into the curriculum."

Dr. Gault also spoke up. "I've known Martha for over twenty years, and there is not a better agency director in our community." Martha was a little embarrassed and frankly surprised by his praise. He had never said such complimentary things to her, though he had always been supportive, ever since her student days. "I'm fortunate to be on the board of directors for Helping Hands," he continued, "and we're grateful to Martha and her staff for their willingness to be with us today."

Martha introduced herself and the staff to the class. She began the presentation with a short introduction to the concept of interprofessional education while explaining why this particular model of practice was the best fit for their work. She also shared some history of interprofessional education and practice from the UK and Australia, where it had been flourishing for decades.

"Interprofessional education is not a new idea," Martha shared. "In fact, it's been around for quite a while. We in the United States like to think we have the market cornered on best practices, but I think we have much to learn from our colleagues around the world."

Martha continued to lay a foundation of knowledge brick by brick. "The World Health Organization defines interprofessional education as education that occurs when students from two or more professions learn about, from, and with each other to enable effective collaboration and, in the case of this program, improve health outcomes. Once students understand how to work interprofessionally, they are ready to enter the workplace as a member of a collaborative practice team. This is a key step in moving health systems from fragmentation to a position of coordinated strength," Martha said. "The key words for me in this definition are 'learn about, from, and with each other' and 'collaborative practice team.' There is undoubtedly going to be a growing trend toward collaborative practice," Martha continued, "for example, in the ways in which the health care system addresses the needs of the Baby Boomers as they age." She could see heads nodding in agreement throughout the class.

Martha told the class that while her agency had always prided itself on their ability to work as a team, adding nurses to the mix along with a very different program was new to all of them. "I'll let the staff fill you in on specifics of their jobs and their work as a team, but let me say now that this venture has been incredibly rewarding for me, as I have the chance to grow as a professional too," she stated.

Fortunately, the class was a three-hour, one day per week course, which gave Melissa and Katie the chance to share what they had learned from one another. They also provided anecdotal evidence of progress they had seen among clients due to their collaboration on cases. Martha chuckled when Professor Gault politely interrupted to remind students that "though stories are often instructive, the plural of anecdote is not data."

Melissa, who was also a former student of Dr. Gault, nodded and moved on. "I've always felt a little frustrated with the fragmentation I see in social services," Melissa offered. "I now have a much better working knowledge of medical issues and treatment options for babies and new mothers." Melissa emphasized that interprofessional collaboration wasn't just about stepping out of the way and letting program partners perform certain tasks but making an effort to better understand the roles and responsibilities of all program service providers.

Katie offered her perspective on the benefits of interprofessional practice. "I learned more about caring for the whole person, body, mind, and spirit, but also the importance of including family in health decisions and being more aware of community-level issues and neighborhood effects on health and well-being," she said. "Honestly, before participating in this program I often felt that these issues were beyond the scope of my practice and not my responsibility. But since I'm on a team with social workers, we now see everything each of us does as our responsibility."

After the presentation, the students had multiple questions for Melissa and Katie and a few for Martha as well. Much of the conversation centered around the tendency to privilege one's own discipline over the other, and the ethical consideration, as one student put it, to effectively argue for one's professional perspective as part of good practice.

A social work major raised his hand. "I'm really curious about boundaries between the clients and the team," he said. "It always seems to me that social work is more about forming relationships and taking the time to do that more than most medical professions do."

Katie smiled and turned to Melissa. "Why don't you tell him how we've dealt with that one?" Melissa laughed and began the story of the first case she and Katie had together.

"One thing we found out quickly is that we needed to compromise in order to get through my need to do a thorough background and intake and Katie's need to get all the necessary medical information quickly!" Melissa said with a grin. "It's not that Katie didn't want to establish a good working relationship with our client; she was simply used to being in a hurry and having a huge caseload of patients to see. I have always been fortunate to work more intensively with smaller caseloads, for example, with evacuees after Hurricane Katrina. That allowed me to get to know my clients really well," she said, "and in the end, serve them more effectively."

"Since then," Katie interjected, "I've become accustomed to making longer home visits, being offered food, watching videos of the children in our families, and truly focusing on the whole picture rather than just the immediate medical needs. My boundaries are definitely different now because my role is different. But Melissa has really impressed upon me the importance of building trust with our families, and that doesn't happen in a fifteen-minute visit."

Martha couldn't help but jump in. "I think what I've witnessed is that Katie and Melissa have become like mentors to some of the young moms in the program," she said. "In fact, though we have a mentor component to the program, we have just started to include mentor training for our staff as well. It's more than the old typical case management and referral that was so prevalent in our jobs before," Martha finished.

When they returned to Helping Hands after their guest lecture that afternoon, Martha was relieved to see that there was no line outside the door. Nothing grieved her more than having to close the doors with people waiting to receive a bag of groceries, some clothes from the pantry, or assistance with utilities. However, when they entered, the lobby was standing room only, with Julia doing her best to organize the sign-in sheet and maintain some semblance of order. The Great Recession, as it was now being called, rumbled on.

On February 17 Martha picked up the morning paper and read, at least by some accounts, that the United States was teetering on the brink of collapse. As he had promised during the campaign, President Obama pushed for a $787 billion stimulus package that was intended to jump-start the economy. Some conservative columnists were calling the American Recovery and Reinvestment Act (ARRA) "a financial boondoggle that would send the U.S. deficit to catastrophic heights." Turning the page, Martha was surprised to read an opinion from Joseph Stiglitz, a Nobel-prize winning economist, that the ARRA did not go far enough, and that it sorely underestimated what it would take to get the economy back on its feet. The polarization of opinion in the paper matched the political environment in Washington, D.C., and many state houses.

Over the next few weeks, details about the stimulus plan became more clear. About one-third of the total, $282 billion, would be in the form of tax breaks to workers, homeowners, and business owners. Another huge number, about $150 billion, would go to states to help them battle looming budget deficits and address educational needs. Martha attempted to get a handle on what seemed like a dizzying array of programs: billion-dollar increases in Pell grants and college work-study programs, almost $30 billion in jobless benefits extended to the long-term unemployed, an $87 billion increase in federal funding for Medicaid, and what would eventually turn out to be almost 30,000 projects intended to revamp the energy sector, modernize medical-records systems, enhance the transportation infrastructure, and promote medical research.

After receiving a $250 check from the government in the mail and noticing that her payroll taxes had been reduced, Martha brought the subject of ARRA's effectiveness up with Dr. Gault the next time they spoke. It didn't take long for her to know where he stood on the issue.

"Well, as you've noticed, Martha, a good chunk of ARRA comes in the form of tax cuts, which just aren't as effective at stimulating the economy as brick-and-mortar projects. Do you remember the section in the policy class that discussed the Great Depression?"

"I took that class over twenty years ago, professor, but I do remember the information you provided about the impact of the WPA, and how the Social Security Act provided a foundation for our welfare state."

"That would be my point, Martha! At its height, WPA projects employed about one out of every ten Americans. If we updated that number, it would equal about 13 million jobs right now. But best estimates indicate that maybe one million jobs will come about due to ARRA."

"Well that figure would certainly support the argument that ARRA isn't doing enough," replied Martha, keeping in mind the large numbers of unemployed that continued to seek assistance from Helping Hands.

"And that brings me to my other point," Professor Gault continued. "Unlike the Social Security Act, which provided a foundation for a strengthened safety net into the future, ARRA is designed to give a short-term boost to the economy. There's nothing in it to address critical shortcomings in our economy, like the lack of paid leave for new parents or caretakers or a system of childcare for working households. As soon as all the money is spent next year, it's just going to fade away. In my mind, it was a critical political mistake by the new administration."

Martha wasn't sure how much she agreed with her former professor. In her mind, President Obama had placed an emphasis on getting a stimulus package signed as soon as possible and had probably gotten as much as he could from a hostile Republican opposition. Regardless, her conversation with Dr. Gault made two things perfectly clear: President Obama wasn't going to enjoy a honeymoon, even from his supporters, and large numbers of people would probably continue to seek assistance from Helping Hands into the foreseeable future.

June 2009

After a Saturday board meeting, Martha asked Robert if she could speak to him privately. "Robert," Martha began, "I have to talk with you about the loan program your business operates. We've had a client come in this week who shared their experience with the program."

"Sure," Robert said. "Is there a problem?"

"As a matter of fact, there is," Martha replied. "A woman came in to Helping Hands the other day after some personal setbacks and an unexpected ambulance bill. She had some medical bills for her daughter that needed to be paid and got behind on her auto loan payment. Her daughter had a severe asthma attack and had to be taken to the ER."

"I'm sorry to hear that," Robert interjected.

"The point is," Martha continued, "when she tried to take her daughter to the hospital, the car wouldn't start. She had to call an ambulance, and that resulted in a costly bill."

"And let me guess," Robert cut in, "it was one of my cars."

"Exactly," Martha said, reminded again of the quick mind that Robert possessed. "As she explained it, her engine had been turned off by your company for a lapsed payment. I wasn't even aware that sort of thing could be done."

"Well," Robert said, "we're the only auto dealer in town that installs an auto shut-off program on cars that we finance." Martha clearly looked perplexed. "Listen," Robert continued, "I'm sorry to hear about her problems, and I hope her daughter is okay. But we don't know the circumstances of our customers when we electronically shut off the ignition for non-payment. I mean, the customers sign on the dotted line and know what they're getting into before they leave the lot."

Martha tried to keep her cool. "I understand that you can't control what happens to people once they leave your lot, Robert. But you have to know that people who purchase cars under those circumstances are already desperate. She showed us her loan papers, and the interest rate is really high. You must know that charging that sort of interest rate is going to reduce the

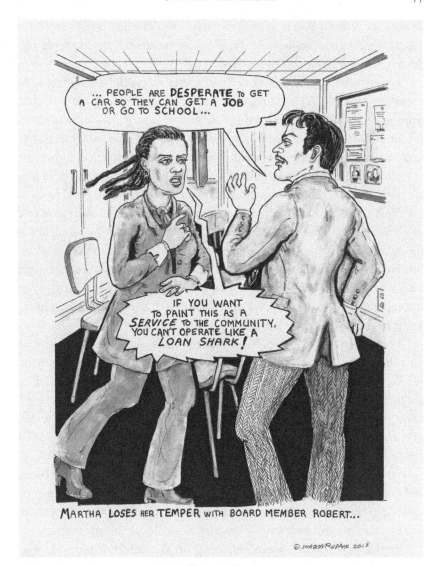

MARTHA LOSES HER TEMPER WITH BOARD MEMBER ROBERT...

likelihood that low-income customers can pay back the loan," Martha said. She could feel her face heating up.

But Robert was heating up as well. "You're right, Martha. People are desperate—they're desperate to get a car so they can get a job or go to school or whatever, and their credit is so bad they can't get a car loan from a bank. We're willing to give them a loan, but we have to cover our risks. It's that simple. In the past we used to have to pay a repo company to find cars when borrowers stopped making payments, but since we started using the ignition devices, we've been able to reduce the number of customers that don't pay. And that's just good business. And it allows us to extend loans to people who otherwise wouldn't be able to purchase a car."

"I have to be honest with you, Robert," Martha said, "it feels more like predatory lending, taking advantage of people's horrible situations, than helping people who need a hand up. And to be honest, it's really not consistent with the mission of Helping Hands. The fact that someone had to seek our help as a result of a board member's business practices has simply never happened before." Martha knew that her anger had gotten the best of her with that last comment, but it was the truth, and she felt she had to say it.

"Wait a minute, I resent what you're implying, Martha!" Robert answered in a heated tone. "First of all, the action that contributed to the problem was the failure of the customer to pay her bills on time and meet her perfectly legal contractual obligations. And second, how many people have been able to get a car and get themselves ahead because I—not some bank or charity—was willing to give them a loan when others wouldn't? You wouldn't even know about all those people!"

"I hear what you're saying, Robert, but she was three weeks late, waiting for a check from her new job that would have allowed her to make a payment. All she needed was a little more time. And you're right, I don't know all of the people in your program, but I do know that none of them are better off having to pay 170% annual interest, which is the rate that was charged on her title loan. If you want to paint this as a service to the community, then you can't operate like a loan shark!"

Robert was having none of it. "You know what, I'm sitting on this board and donating my time as a courtesy. I don't need to come here and have my ethics questioned by someone who doesn't know the first damn thing about what it takes to run a business!" With that, he brusquely left the room.

Martha stood there, quietly reflecting on the confrontation. She certainly wished it hadn't gotten so heated, but she was outraged over Robert's comments. Did he really think he was helping people rather than taking advantage of them?

Martha's cell phone rang. It was Allen. She was so mad she thought about just letting it ring, but decided to answer it. "Honey, what time are you heading home today?"

Martha took a deep breath. "I'll be ready to go in about thirty minutes, but I need to talk to Carlene about a very unpleasant meeting I just had with a board member. She couldn't come to the meeting today, but I know she would want me to fill her in." Allen didn't ask for any further details, so she decided not to tell him what had just transpired with Robert.

Carlene had a different take when they had a chance to chat a few minutes later. "While I see your point, Martha, I do wish things hadn't gotten so out of hand," she offered. "We knew he was a businessman when we made him the offer to join the board. And regardless, Robert has connections in town that can help or hurt us if he chooses to make an issue out of this. Did he say he was quitting?"

"He didn't, but I would be surprised if he stayed after this. And honestly, in spite of his connections, I'm not sure I want him on the board. Think of it, Carlene, we actually had a person seek our help as a result of his program," Martha replied. "As if things aren't bad enough with this recession, we now have to contend with the fallout from the predatory actions of one of our board members?" Martha said while shaking her head on the phone.

Carlene let the comment hang on the line and then said, "Let me follow up with him. I'm a business owner too, and I know the challenges that come with trying to make a profit while covering payroll and expenses."

"But Carlene, your business doesn't take advantage of people and set them up for failure. It doesn't force a struggling mom into medical debt because you shut down her car."

"Martha," Carlene replied in a calm tone of voice, "I know you're passionate and that's why Helping Hands has survived over the years. You know I don't mean to be critical of that passion, but Robert's world really is different."

"I know Carlene, and I'm not blind to the practical realities of the for-profit world. But it has to be possible to make a profit without exploiting people. Exorbitant interest rates aren't necessary; hidden fees aren't necessary. Simply give a loan, charge a reasonable interest to cover your administrative costs and bring a profit, and work with people if they get behind. That seems to me to be a reasonable expectation if you deliberately court people who have financial troubles."

Carlene knew Martha was on a roll and just listened.

"I didn't get into this with Robert," Martha continued, "but I did some research on the issue of ignition shut-off switches. I read about a woman who tried to take her car into another county to seek shelter from her abusive husband. The car stopped when she crossed the "allowable distance" and prevented her from seeking safety. People's lives are complicated, and if you're going to work with the folks we do, you have to know that and not take advantage of them."

"I know," said Carlene sympathetically. "It's a complicated world. I guess I just don't want us to, you know, let the perfect be the enemy of the good." Martha knew her friend and board member was giving her good advice.

Three days later Martha received Robert's resignation letter via certified mail.

Discussion Questions

1. President Obama won the November 4, 2008, election in an electoral landslide, and the Democratic Party earned majorities in both the House and Senate. As the new chief executive, President Obama quickly pushed through a stimulus proposal (ARRA) that included over $200 billion in tax cuts. In lieu of these tax cuts, what social program(s) do you think it would have been important to fund? Explain your reasoning.
2. Martha participates in an eviction blockade to protest the predatory lending experienced by the Johnsons, her elderly neighbors. Have you ever heard about eviction protests taking place in your community? Would you be willing to participate in such a protest in support of a family member, friend, or neighbor? Why or why not? Are there other methods that you think would be more appropriate and/or effective?
3. The chapter makes a strong case for the benefits of interprofessional education and practice. But what are some of the potential drawbacks (for example, between the "medical expert" model in the health fields and the "strengths-based model" favored by the profession of social work)?
4. What do you think of the way Martha responded to and addressed Robert's business practices? If you were executive director of a community agency, how would you respond if you found out that a board member's business practices had caused economic hardship for one of your clients?

Suggested Readings

Cannon, M., & Preble, C. (2014, June 15). The other veterans scandal. *New York Times*. Retrieved from http://www.nytimes.com/2014/06/16/opinion/the-other-veterans-scandal.html.

Corkery, M., & Silver-Greenberg, J. (2014, September 24). Miss a payment? Good luck moving that car. *New York Times*.

Crawford, K. (2011). *Interprofessional collaboration in social work practice*. Thousand Oaks, CA: SAGE.

Desmond, M. (2016). *Evicted: Poverty and profit in an American city*. New York: Crown.

Dyson, M. E. (2016). *The Black presidency: Barack Obama and the politics of race in America*. New York: Houghton, Mifflin, Harcourt.

Grunwald, M. (2012). *The new, New Deal: The hidden story of change in the Obama era*. New York: Simon & Schuster.

Kroll, A. (2009, May 26). The greatest swindle ever sold. *The Nation*. Retrieved from http://thenation.com/doc/20090608/kroll/print

Margolis, M., & Noonan, M. (2016). *The worst president in history: The legacy of Barack Obama*. New York: Victory Books.

Mian, A., & Amir, S. (2015). *House of debt: How they (and you) caused the Great Recession, and how we can prevent it from happening again*. Chicago: University of Chicago Press.

Phillips, D. (2016, July 7). Suicide rates among vets has risen sharply since 2001. *New York Times*. Retrieved from http://www.nytimes.com/2016/07/08/us/suicide-rate-among-veterans-has-risen-sharply-since-2001.html?_r=0

Rosenberg, J. (2010). *The concise encyclopedia of the Great Recession: 2007–2010*. Lanham, MD: Scarecrow Press.

Sawyer, M., Bowering, K., Frost, L., & Lynch, J. (2013). Effectiveness of nurse home-visiting programs for disadvantaged families: Results of a natural experiment. *Health Services Research, 3*(4).

Sicko. (2007). New York: Weinstein Co. Home Entertainment.

Silver-Greenberg, J., & Corkery, M. (2014, December 25). Rise in loans linked to cars is hurting poor. *New York Times*.

Todd, C., & Gawiser, S. (2009). *How Barack Obama won: A state-by-state guide to the historic 2008 presidential election*. New York: Vintage.

6

A Healthy Start

MARCH 2010: MARTHA walked out of the social work building at River City U feeling inspired. She had just led an enthusiastic group of undergraduates in a spirited discussion about the early work of the Children's Bureau. None of the students had heard of the Children's Bureau prior to becoming social work majors, and they were amazed to hear about the success of the "Baby Saving" campaign that workers at the bureau had organized. The effort eventually involved millions of women around the country in birth registration campaigns, and millions more were helped by the educational pamphlets that the Children's Bureau produced related to maternal and child health. The small staff also responded in writing to over 100,000 letters they received each year. The campaign, and progress in other areas like public health and sanitation, cut the infant mortality rate in half over a twenty-year period. Martha noted that it was such a signal achievement that demographers refer to the era as the "American Mortality Transition." Martha used the campaign waged by these early social workers to reinforce the importance of a macro-focus in confronting social problems.

Martha's decision to teach a class had been years in the making. Dr. Gault had asked many times if she would be interested in teaching social work courses as an adjunct instructor. Though she had always been interested in the idea, her work at Helping Hands and keeping up with the twins consumed all her time. Now, with Brandon and Jessie in college and her funding situation stable with the Early Intervention Home Visiting grant, Martha agreed to teach a social problems and policy course at her alma mater. Though she had supervised social work interns for years at Helping Hands, Martha found that she really enjoyed teaching groups of students in a classroom setting. She was only a couple of months into the semester and had not yet completed much grading, but the classroom discussions had been lively and the students impressed her with their energy and commitment to social change. It was also a plus to be able to tap into the expertise of colleagues from an array of social work fields. To her surprise, the most vexing part of the experience was learning the electronic system through which tests, readings, assignments, and grades were administered. Martha remembered her first semester at River City U in the 1980s had included demonstrations on how to use the Dewey decimal card files to find books and articles. And when she mentioned threading microfiche into a manual scanner to find articles, the students returned blank stares. Most had never heard the word "microfiche" before.

As an adjunct instructor Martha decided to imbibe in the student schedule and take Brandon and Jessie to Washington, D.C., for spring break. Over the course of her career she had attended numerous conferences in the nation's capitol and reveled in the museum culture that was everywhere present. To prep for the trip, Martha read a book titled *Black Men Built the Capitol: Discovering African-American History In and Around Washington*. The book was a fascinating collection of stories about the important roles Blacks played in building the White House and many of the historic landmarks along the Mall and around the city. In addition to the more well-known monuments, she took the kids to the Frederick Douglass National Historic Site and the Mary McLeod Bethune Memorial in Lincoln Park (the first monument to honor an African American woman in a public park), and even had the kids take pictures of the Banneker Boundary Stone, named after Benjamin Banneker, a self-educated African American who helped survey and map out Washington, D.C. Both of the kids seemed to be especially moved by the African American Civil War Memorial, a moving paean to the two hundred thousand African-American soldiers who had fought in the Union army during the Civil War. Brandon was studying to be an athletic trainer and was not a politically minded person, but he was angered that much of what they had experienced had never been mentioned in his high school history classes.

Jessie was quick to respond. "That's the way history is, B. It focuses on the winners and always ignores the contributions that we and other minority groups have made."

For once, Brandon didn't answer his sister with a glib remark.

"You know," interjected Martha, "I remember going to see a movie called *Glory* when I was pregnant with you two. It was about the first all-Black company in the Union army and the racism they experienced from their own side."

"Is that the one with Denzel, Mama?" asked Jessie.

"Yes, Denzel and Morgan Freeman," Martha answered. "And let me tell you," Martha said with emphasis, "Denzel was looking good in that movie!"

"He's still looking good," Jessie quickly confirmed.

Martha shared an idea. "I'll put the film in my Netflix queue and we can make a movie night of it sometime." As soon as she said it, it hit her how infrequently the kids were home together. Though they had been out of the house for almost three years, she was still adjusting to the change.

A week after returning from her spring break sojourn, Martha picked up the paper and read that Congress had just passed the Patient Protection and Affordable Care Act (ACA), or what was already being referred to derisively by political opponents as "Obamacare." She remembered that as a candidate President Obama had promised to work on health care reform and early in his term the previous year had sponsored a White House "Health Summit" that involved various stakeholders in the health care arena. He had also appointed Kansas governor Kathleen Sebelius to head the White House Office for Health Reform. But after that, perhaps because of the two foreign wars he had inherited and the continuing difficulties posed by the economic downturn, President Obama seemed to cede leadership on the issue to Congress. Martha became further disillusioned when a "Medicare for All" system was taken off the negotiation table and when she read that Republicans were making efforts to assure that federal funding for abortion was not included. She remembered how the Clinton health care reform effort had foundered in the early 1990s and assumed the same thing would happen again, especially when the Republican-controlled House voted to repeal the ACA in January.

She was wrong.

As the newspaper article stated, Obama and House Speaker Nancy Pelosi kept up the pressure, and on March 21 the Senate version of the bill passed by a narrow margin in the House—without the vote of a single Republican lawmaker.

Reading on, Martha was perplexed by the tone of the articles. Despite the enormity of the health care problem in the United States, with more than 50 million Americans uninsured and almost 30 million underinsured, the articles seemed oddly ambivalent about the importance of the legislation. One of them quoted from Republican majority leader John Boehner's angry speech denouncing the legislation: "This bill is not what the American people need nor what our constituents want." Martha couldn't remember another instance in modern American history when a significant piece of legislation had passed without *any* support from one of the two major political parties. She made a mental note to look up headlines from around the country to get a better sense of how other papers were covering the ACA's passage.

The articles in the *River City Star* provided solid information on the basics of the ACA. The primary part of the bill would begin in 2014, though provisions of it would start later that year. Martha looked the early provisions over; they seemed to make sense. They prohibited restrictions on lifetime dollar limits on coverage and exclusions for those under nineteen with pre-existing conditions, allowed dependent children to stay on their parents' plans until age twenty-six (as the paper put it, "because young adults were having trouble finding jobs"), and barred insurers from requiring co-pays for preventive care. These provisions would no doubt have a huge impact on her students, many of whom were uninsured during the course of their studies.

The legislation also required employers with more than fifty employees to provide coverage or face penalties, expanded funding for community health centers, established an "individual mandate" to purchase coverage or pay penalties, and provided subsidies for individuals and families to purchase affordable coverage through a health insurance market place.

These were certainly significant changes, but it was the change to the Medicaid program that caught her eye. Over her entire social work career, Martha had worked with low-income populations. Though some had received coverage through Medicaid, one of President Lyndon Johnson's War on Poverty programs passed along with Medicare in 1965, the income threshold to be eligible to receive Medicaid in Martha's state was so low that many of the working poor who received services at Helping Hands simply did without health insurance. Though poor, they made too much money to qualify for Medicaid and, like millions of the working class, were not offered or could not afford health insurance through their employers. This meant no regular doctor visits, no consistent use of needed medications, and, often, a reliance on expensive emergency rooms for required care.

Under the ACA, however, Medicaid eligibility was going to be expanded to a point above the poverty line. The federal government would pay for 100% of the costs in the first three years of expansion and 90% of the costs after 2020. It reminded Martha of the good deal the feds gave state governments with regard to the Food Stamps program: payment of 100% of the actual benefits and 50% of state administrative costs. Reading these figures it suddenly hit her: the low-income clients that Helping Hands served would all be eligible for Medicaid coverage! A huge problem that Helping Hands had wrestled with for years was gone in the stroke of Obama's pen. Well, she thought to herself, when the ACA took full effect in 2014, anyway.

At work, Martha got a report from Melissa, Hayley, and John about Nola Patterson, a twenty-seven-year-old married client with a premature baby. Nola, who had spent time in the foster care system, had her first child when she was seventeen and using methamphetamine. The Department of Children's Services (DHS) had removed the infant from her care when the baby tested positive for drugs at birth. Her parental rights were terminated when she was unable to successfully complete drug rehabilitation within the timelines required by federal law. Now she was married to DJ, age twenty-nine, a cook at a local restaurant. Nola had been drug-free since she completed rehab at age twenty. That had been a tremendous accomplishment, as it required Nola to spend time in a homeless shelter after extricating herself from a dealer who sometimes acted as a pimp in payment for drugs. She had fond memories of her grandmother cooking when she was younger and decided to go to culinary school and start a small catering business when she finished the treatment program. She and DJ met while in school and got married when Nola was twenty-five. Since the child she had when she was seventeen was premature, and due to her past history with child protective services, Nola was considered "high risk" by the DHS and referred while she was still pregnant. In spite of her clear progress over the past few years, the DHS caseworker wanted staff at Helping Hands to work with Nola and DJ. It helped that both Nola and DJ were receptive to the support that the Helping Hands program offered. The staff had just completed their second home visit, and Hayley and John were debating her case.

On the first home visit, Nola had complained that the baby never seemed to sleep for more than an hour or two and was always crying. John discussed acid reflux as a common cause of colic among babies, but just to be safe he decided to give the baby, whom they had named Joshua, a quick exam. He immediately recognized a bilateral hernia and helped Nola make an appointment with a pediatric surgeon. The news from the surgeon was mixed: yes, the hernia could be fixed, but given his diminutive size the more time they could give to let Joshua grow, the more likely the surgery would be a success. This meant Nola was left home all day with a baby that was in constant distress and often crying.

Hayley was clearly troubled by John's more pessimistic opinion of Nola's potential. "Look," she argued, "I know I'm just an intern, but it's been seven years since she had a drug problem. Why don't we look at *that* track record instead of her distant past? One thing I've learned in my social work classes is to start where the client is, not where they were years ago."

Melissa spoke up, as she was Hayley's direct supervisor for the internship and wanted to push her to think deeper about the case. "Hayley, I hear what you're saying, but we can't deny the stress of caring for a preemie with a hernia either. I agree that she's been stable for a while, but this is a whole new situation for her, right?"

John interjected. "As you noted yourself, Hayley, DJ works a lot of hours, leaving the bulk of the care to Nola." John had done an extended rotation in a neonatal unit prior to joining the home visiting program and had a much more sensitive assessment about the risks. "I've seen lots of families with preemies struggle, and I just can't ignore the warning signs in this case. I'm just trying to be realistic here."

Martha had listened quietly up to this point but now decided to ask some questions before giving them all feedback.

"Hayley, tell me about your observations of Nola. Give me some details about her interactions with the baby, the conditions of the apartment, and anything else you feel is relevant." Martha liked Hayley and saw in her the passion for social justice that she felt as a college student. That passion drew her to social work as a major, and having interns with such enthusiasm always rekindled her own fire.

"Nola was holding the baby when we got there," Hayley began. "She had just fed him and had been rocking him to sleep. She said he can break into screams with the slightest disruption, and she was nervous we'd make that happen." Martha asked if that was her assessment or if Nola had said she was anxious. Hayley replied that it was "a little of both." Nola mentioned DJ had come home recently and had woken Joshua when he shut the door. After that Joshua had cried for hours.

"I think she's also understandably nervous with three professionals coming into her home to check up on her, especially given her history with DCS," Hayley continued. "I know how I'd feel in her shoes."

"What happened after you got there?" asked Martha. "Did the baby stay asleep?"

"No, he woke up when she tried to put him in the crib, which was in the nursery off of the living room," Hayley answered. "She ended up rocking him the entire time we were there. As for the house, it was clean; dishes had been hand-washed and were in the rack drying. She told us she had done some late-night cleaning with DJ the night before. She was dressed nicely but not formally, and it looked like she was taking care of herself and the baby. I certainly didn't notice anything about the house or her appearance that made me worry," she finished, looking over at John for his reaction.

John couldn't help but grin. "All of that is absolutely accurate from my perspective," he said. "However, once we began chatting, it was evident to me that this is a real challenge for Nola, as it would be for anyone, but it's clearly more than she expected. She wasn't planning on a premature baby but was diagnosed with pre-eclampsia. It's a leading cause of premature births, and Joshua was born at thirty-two weeks. His lungs need maturing, and his nervous system is oversensitive. I think when they are able to perform the surgery that's going to help a lot. But I suspect as he gets older he's going to be a handful, perhaps hyperactive and overly impulsive. He should grow out of that, but in the meantime, this whole situation puts her and the baby at risk. I can imagine the desire to use substances to cope with this level of stress and sleep deprivation could be pretty powerful." When he finished, Martha asked Melissa for her take on the case.

"Both Hayley and John make good points. I think both of their assessments are accurate. The problem is that we can't agree on the route to take in terms of services for the family," Melissa answered. "We didn't get to see DJ, as he was already in for his shift at the restaurant. He is critical to the family's success, and he is, by all accounts, a thoughtful and supportive husband. It's just that he works long hours, which leaves Nola to do the bulk of the care. She really doesn't have too many other supports. Her catering partner is covering the business for now, but Nola's isolation does worry me." Melissa stopped to think and then shared the divergent paths of care for which John and Hayley were pushing.

"Hayley feels we should do more wraparound services, find a support group for mothers with preemies, look into day care options equipped for babies like Joshua, and reach out to Nola's NA sponsor for additional help," she said.

"That feels much more strengths-based to me, rather than deficit-based," said Martha, "and that is certainly the social work perspective in general. Capitalizing on natural supports while acknowledging needs is a great idea."

John chimed in with his concerns. "I honestly think CPS should just keep this as an open case and that she should be forced to attend NA more often than she has," he said. "She hasn't gone since the baby was born six weeks ago, and that is a warning sign to me."

"But how is she supposed to go if she has no child care, John?" exclaimed Hayley in an exasperated tone. "This feels like a punishment or at best an overly paternalistic response. How is DCS ever the best option for a family? They lose kids in foster care; have deaths on their watch. The news is filled with stories from around the country every year," she said. "I, for one, want to get DCS off her back and have her see us as helpful, not monitoring her, or waiting for her to mess up!" Hayley's frustration was evident in her voice and her face.

"Well, if we don't pay attention to the risks and she's not being forced to use NA, who's going to be sure she stays clean and doesn't neglect the baby?" John responded calmly. Martha was thankful for John's mature and professional way of responding to Hayley's energetic assessments. Clearly, the former ER nurse didn't rattle easily.

"The news is also filled with examples of abuse and neglect that went unaddressed," he continued. "I don't want to ignore something that could lead to bigger problems later."

As Martha listened, she reflected on the age-old battle between the medical model of diagnosing and treating a problem, which put the power in the hands of the professional, and the social work model, which focused on strengths and sought to empower clients to make needed changes. Like John, Martha had worked in a hospital ER and knew from experience that nursing and social work often disagreed on the approach to take. Nevertheless, she was hopeful the focus on interprofessional education would drop some of the walls and help each side to see the benefits of the other's perspective.

Her response to the debate tried to start that process. "John, I totally understand where you're coming from, and of course, her risk of using again with a demanding new baby is an obvious concern. We should definitely discuss that real possibility with her and let *her tell us* what she needs to stay clean. That allows us to still acknowledge her success and learn how she has managed her sobriety over the past few years."

John agreed that made great sense. "I would be okay with that. I simply don't want us to ignore a potentially unsafe situation."

"Thanks for being open to that, John," Martha replied. "I'd also like to know if you would be willing to contact the surgeon and see what he thinks about scheduling the procedure sooner rather than later. If this was a best-case scenario we could wait as long as needed but I think we would all agree that this is a special case."

"I could do that," John replied. "The last time we talked, the surgeon said every extra day would help, and it's been a few weeks. I'll see what she says."

Martha next dealt with Hayley's concern that Nola was being too easily condemned. It seemed that Hayley's main problem with John's plan was including DCS as the monitor.

As if reading Martha's mind, Hayley repeated her argument. "I've heard and read way too many stories about overzealous caseworkers, typically not with social work degrees, jumping to conclusions and overacting to a client's *potential* problem. How could we ever establish a trusting relationship with Nola if our first response is to ask CPS to keep an open case on her? I'd prefer that we provide education for her to deal with this situation, and maybe some respite care so she can have a break from the stress."

"You're right, Hayley," Martha replied. "We absolutely need to establish a trusting relationship with Nola and DJ, one that supports them and is based on the belief that they are doing a good job raising their son." She smiled, "Keep on standing up for your clients, Hayley, but also remember that problems, even potential problems, can't be ignored as we try to focus on strengths."

Melissa smiled. She had worked with Martha for a number of years and considered Martha more of a mentor than a boss. She had a way of dealing with problems that Melissa hoped to emulate, and no matter how stressful things got, she had never seen Martha lose her cool. Melissa was thankful to be working full-time at Helping Hands, and she told Martha so as she led her team back to their office to set up their schedule with Nola. Though Martha graciously accepted the compliment, she thought about her interaction with Robert and resolved to share that episode with Melissa in the future.

The following week Martha bumped into Dr. Gault in the social work building on her way to teach class. "It's a good time to be teaching social policy, eh Martha?" he quipped with a wry grin.

"It sure is," replied Martha. "As a matter of fact, I'm going to cover the basics about the ACA in class today."

"You know, there's a subtext to that whole story, Martha. It demonstrates the rightward shift in our politics, especially within the Republican Party."

"Because not a single Republican voted for it?" Martha asked.

"That's exactly right. You know, I looked up the vote on Medicare/Medicaid in '65. Thirteen Republican Senators and seventy Republican House members voted for it. That was a majority of the Republican House members. Can you believe it?"

"That's a striking change, Alvin, but it begs the question, what caused the shift to the Right?"

"That's a question for the ages, Martha! But unless we both want to be late to class, I suggest we reserve it for another time."

"You know where to find me," Martha replied with a smile as they both hustled down the hall.

When the students had settled down, Martha began. "I know we were supposed to talk about the minimum wage today, but in light of the Affordable Care Act being passed, I thought it would be important to discuss it right away."

The students nodded, and Martha continued.

"How many of you have been following the ACA in the news?" A smattering of hands went up. It was clear that the basic components of the new health law would have to be covered. Martha spent the next forty-five minutes discussing the health care problem in the United States, with some 50 million people uninsured and millions more underinsured, and the basic outline of the plan. She described the ways in which the new law would have an impact on students and low-income and working populations. Martha was surprised to find out that many students were unaware of the policy change that allowed students to remain on their parents' health plans until the age of twenty-six. She then devoted the remainder of class for student questions.

One of the students fired off a good question right away. "You mentioned that the feds are going to pay for states to expand Medicaid. Are they going to pay for the whole thing forever?"

Martha had to look down at her notes to answer this one. "Let me see, ah yes, here it is. From 2014 through 2016, the feds are going to pay for 100% of the expansion. Then from 2017 through 2019 they will pay about 95%. After that, they will pay 90% of the costs."

"That's a pretty good deal, isn't it?" asked the student.

"Yes," said Martha. "It's a very good deal. I think the intention was to be so generous that states would be crazy not to take the offer."

Another hand went up. "My dad says that it's just going to be a bait-and-switch tactic by the federal government, and that even if they do pay for it, taxes are going to be raised so that a bunch of freeloaders can get health care. He's also against the government forcing people to buy health care."

Another student immediately responded. "The government forces people to buy car insurance, and home insurance, why not health insurance?"

The first student shrugged and said, "Hey, don't shoot the messenger!" The class laughed and Martha felt the tension in the room diminish.

Another student reflected on the comment. "I've heard the same thing," she said, "but from the information we just covered it sounds like people with incomes up to 400% of the poverty line will be eligible for subsidies, right?"

Martha nodded affirmatively.

"Then it seems evident to me that the vast majority of people who are going to receive assistance are working people with incomes above poverty, and businesses that provide coverage for employees," said the student in response. "They don't sound like freeloaders to me."

Just for a moment, the room went quiet.

July 2010

Martha and Allen decided to visit Brandon in Flagstaff, Arizona, while he was completing an internship in physical therapy. The cool temperatures and the smell of pine trees that seemed to pervade the entire city was a welcome reprieve from the intense summer heat of River City. A high point of the trip had been a visit to the Grand Canyon. Brandon had taken them by the hands and made them close their eyes as they approached the lookout point on the rim. Martha would never forget the awe-inspiring sight she saw upon opening her eyes. It looked like the pictures she had seen, but the enormity of its scope surpassed anything she had ever seen. She looked at Allen and saw in his open-mouthed amazement the same wonder and inspiration that she now felt.

In the morning, Martha picked up the complementary paper at the hotel and read that what was being called the Dodd-Frank Act had just passed. The act, though opposed by many in Congress, was championed by President Obama as a way to curb the excesses of Wall Street investment practices and reduce the risks of the financial system on the US economy. Martha immediately thought that Melissa would be happy to hear this news, though she would probably say that it was "too little and too late" to help the millions who had been hung out to dry in the continuing recession. The end of the article quoted from a Harvard law professor by the name of Elizabeth Warren who urged the creation of an agency that would monitor industry practices and represent the interests of consumers.

In October, Melissa and Martha sat with a visibly upset Hayley in the break room after hours, attempting to work through everyone's disappointment and strategize next steps that would need to be taken. Earlier that day, the team had heard Joshua, the baby of Nola and DJ, crying as they approached the apartment for their scheduled visit. After ringing the bell and pounding on the door for ten minutes, they had the apartment manager open the door. Nola was nowhere to be found, and the baby had not been changed or fed. John insisted they call CPS when neither Nola nor DJ could be reached by phone. Hayley's frustration and disappointment was palpable. "I advocated for her; I trusted her and worked hard to get resources for her, and then she puts that little boy at risk!" she exclaimed while holding back tears.

Hayley had been hired by the program upon completion of her degree in social work, and she and John had remained part of the team for Nola and DJ's case.

Fortunately, after a few hours, DJ returned their calls and met them at the CPS office. After an interview and promises not to leave the baby with Nola alone, the CPS worker allowed him to take Joshua home. The presence of Helping Hands caseworkers in their lives was clearly a factor in the decision, and despite the tense situation, DJ expressed his appreciation for their assistance. However, Nola had now jeopardized their chance to maintain custody. DJ called at 4 PM and said he still had not heard from Nola. Everyone suspected she had begun using again, and while DJ said he had not seen signs of that, he admitted he had been working longer hours to bring in extra money as Nola's partner had left the catering business.

Joshua was now seven months old, but Helping Hands had stayed involved with the family. Typically, their cases were meant to close in six months, but due to the health issues Joshua faced as a premature baby and the stress Nola and DJ faced in managing both him and work, Melissa had received permission from their grant manager in Washington, D.C., to add them to a long-term case list. Given what had happened, it was fortunate that they were still working with the family.

"We all feel the way you do Hayley," said Melissa. "Relapse is part of the process of working in the area of addiction. It's hard not to take it personally after we've been so close to the family, but we have to separate emotionally from this and figure out how we can help at this point."

"I hate to say I told you so . . ." John began.

"Then don't," Hayley quickly retorted. "She was doing well, and the services we provided for her really seemed to be working." Martha noted Hayley's sharp tone and intervened immediately.

"Both of you were right about her," Martha stated, hoping it would defray the tension. "That's why we stayed involved for so long," she said while looking at them both. "But she was clearly under a lot of stress, and it was just too much for her to manage. Let's think about this. Her business went under during the economic crisis, leaving no choice but for DJ to work longer hours and for Nola to do the bulk of child care. Joshua's health problems made ordinary child care impossible, so she couldn't go out and find another job. This increased her isolation and made her feel terrible. I know you all saw some of this coming, and you did your best to provide her resources, like Narcotics Anonymous and a support group for mothers, but I'm not sure we could have predicted she would ever just take off and leave Joshua like that."

"And now our immediate priority is helping DJ as much as we can," Melissa said. "I hope the police actually find Nola or she returns on her own, because I'm concerned for her safety. If she's using again, she could have gotten herself into a dangerous situation. Poor DJ must be out of his mind with worry."

"With your permission," John replied, "I'd like to go over this evening and check on them, without the whole team." John was a father himself, and he imagined how he would feel if he was in DJ's shoes. "I think having another dad to talk to might be helpful," he continued. "I have to say you social workers have rubbed off on me; I've developed some pretty good counseling skills I wouldn't have otherwise." He looked at Hayley after he spoke, and it was clear the compliment helped ease the tension between them.

Martha and Melissa agreed with John's plan. "In the meantime," said Melissa, "the three of us will stay here and think of some short-term plans for child care so that DJ can still work. We'll also see if we can help locate Nola," Melissa said, her face showing her sadness and concern. Ruth entered the room and was apprised of the situation.

"I think it would be a good idea to talk to her neighbor, Joanie," Hayley began. "She's been there when we've gone to visit, and I know she's done some babysitting for them. She might know something; and who knows, she might even be willing to help DJ with child care too," she said.

"Well, it can't hurt to try, Hayley," Melissa replied. "But it's after 5 PM now, and you need to go home and rest, get a break from all this. Watch a funny movie or hang out with some friends. You need to remind yourself that there's more to life than the kind of pain you see with some of our clients."

"Fijate," Ruth offered, "after a hard day teaching in New York, I'd order a calzone as big as a football from this little Italian place on my way home."

Martha chuckled. "You know, when I was first starting out at CPS I would rent an Eddie Murphy movie to chill out after a hard day."

"Who's that?" asked Hayley.

Martha shook her head and laughed. "You Millennials, you're all poor deprived creatures!"

"What?" asked Hayley. "Am I supposed to know him? I mean, I don't think some old movie is gonna do it for me!"

Martha feigned indignance. "You just don't know what you're missing!" she said as Hayley made her way out.

After Hayley left, Martha complimented Melissa on her supervisory skills.

"Well, I had a good model to follow," Melissa responded.

Martha smiled and thanked her.

"Dios mio!" interjected Ruth. "You know, the proper way to share all this love would be over a calzone!"

"You buyin'?" asked Melissa with a grin.

"I just have one question," Martha asked, directing her gaze at Melissa. "Do *you* know who Eddie Murphy is?"

Melissa responded hesitantly. "He's the Dr. Doolittle guy, right?"

Martha shook her head and looked at Ruth. "Let's go get that calzone and set this girl straight!"

One week later, DJ called to say that Nola was home. She had been found by the police passed out in her car in an area where heroin dealing had become prevalent. She had then been taken to a local hospital for observation. After she had stabilized DJ was contacted by the ER social worker to come and pick her up.

A CPS caseworker, Hayley, John, and Melissa met with the family the following day. CPS had continued their investigation and opened a case to monitor the situation. The team learned that Nola had begun the downward slide a few months earlier, purchasing synthetic marijuana as a means to help her relax when DJ worked late. It was clear that DJ had no idea and was both hurt and angry that she had not talked with him about her situation. While Nola had been using marijuana for those months, she indicated that this had been her first use of heroin. The day she left Joshua alone, she had taken him to a store where he had inexplicably thrown a fit. She had been unable to calm him and ended up leaving her groceries in the middle of the checkout line. She felt the eyes of everyone in the store upon her and became overwhelmed. He cried the entire way home. Unable to find a cause for his crying, Nola left him in the apartment to go buy a fix. The heroin caused a serious reaction, and she eventually lost consciousness. When she awoke and realized what had happened, she was overcome with guilt and decided against returning while under the obvious influence of drugs. The situation deteriorated from there. Fortunately, the team had arrived at the apartment that day for their appointment, essentially saving Joshua from potential disaster.

In partnership with Helping Hands, CPS created a plan to address safety for Joshua, Nola's addiction, and the relationship between DJ and Nola. Because Nola had proven unreliable in protecting Joshua, CPS would not allow her to stay with him alone. For the last week their neighbor Joanie had agreed to watch Joshua along with her own toddler, and DJ said his sister would also be willing to help. Nola began intensive outpatient treatment for her addiction at an all-day program at the local mental health center. Due to a contractual arrangement with the Department of Health and Human Services, fees for the service were waived. During the treatment, Joanie and DJ's sister agreed to alternate care for Joshua. Because of Nola's addiction history DJ's family had been standoffish, but this crisis and their love for Joshua brought the family together.

DJ was incredibly grateful for those who came forward to help, but his anger with Nola was palpable. The treatment program Nola attended encouraged DJ to be a part of the counseling, but his job and the need to care for Joshua made that extremely difficult. As he was the only source of income for the family, he took double shifts when he could but, if no other caregiver was available, was required to be home with Joshua whenever Nola was there. Hesitant to ask for additional help, DJ delayed the counseling and put the focus on Nola's getting "her act together."

In a staff meeting, Hayley provided an update on Nola's progress in treatment and details of her conversations with Joanie and DJ's sister about caring for Joshua.

"Nola's remorse is overwhelming her right now," Hayley shared. "She's working the program as the therapist suggests, but she keeps imagining what might have happened to Joshua and just breaks down. She's afraid DJ might leave her and take Joshua away. We need to get the two of them into counseling to deal with this stuff head on." Martha knew that this experience had helped Hayley to have a better understanding of the complicated physical and psychological effects of addiction. Ultimately, it would make her a better social worker and advocate, but, for now, there was no getting around that it was a tough learning experience.

John, with whom DJ had shared some of his anger toward Nola, offered his take. "DJ has had to take on more direct care of Joshua, and I've focused on teaching him how to handle the frequent crying due to Josh's nervous system," he said. "I think he's overwhelmed with all the responsibilities he has, and he's still really angry with Nola. The counselor told him it was okay to express his anger, but if he can't get past it, I think Hayley is right. Things will get out of control real quickly."

Melissa listened intently to the conversation. John and Hayley weren't on the same page often, but it was clear that each had learned from the other. John clearly benefitted from the social work training regarding the therapeutic relationship and counseling skills he got in their joint classes, and Hayley learned that when dealing with a disease such as addiction, the worker has to understand the nature of the illness and use that to make sound judgments about cases.

The meeting ended with plans for Hayley and John to do a home visit when Nola and DJ were home and perhaps refer them to a program that did in-home family therapy to prevent removals of children from the custody of their parents. Couple therapy wasn't actually the purpose of the program, but, in this situation, it was necessary to prevent further harm. Hayley called a friend and former classmate at another community agency to see if they could take a new referral and make this case "fit" their criteria. She told Hayley to make a formal referral with the authorization from CPS. As with the addictions program, her agency had a contract with CPS that would provide services to families free of charge.

Martha scheduled a meeting for the team and the professors working in the interprofessional education program at the university. Nola and DJ were just one of many challenging cases the home visiting program worked with, and she wanted her staff to provide feedback to the nursing and social work programs. Hopefully, the program feedback would help to better inform curriculum and field placements in the future. Though there had been progress, Martha felt there was still a tendency for each profession to persistently cling to its own "territory" or knowledge base. Martha had faith in the concept of interprofessional education and believed that a multidisciplinary service perspective was the best way to address complicated personal and community-level problems.

November 2011

Melissa entered Martha's office and sat in front of her desk. "I need to take a week of vacation, and I need it right away," she stated rather bluntly.

"Oh," said Martha. "Is there an emergency?"

"Not exactly, but I guess it depends on your point of view. Occupy Wall Street was just forced out of Zucotti Park, and me and my partner want to participate in the one here before it gets shut down too. And I think that's going to happen sooner rather than later."

"Why do you think that?" Martha asked.

"Well, the mayor has been trying to get them to relocate from city hall, and when they resisted, he had nearby public bathrooms locked and then sent cleaning crews with high-pressure sprayers to come in late at night. They've soaked the encampment multiple times."

"I read about that," said Martha. "But he claimed it was because the encampments were a danger to public health."

"Yeah, right," came Melissa's caustic reply.

"Is there anything big scheduled for the program in the coming week?" Martha asked.

"Not really," said Melissa. "We haven't had a referral in the last week, and John and Hayley can handle the follow-up visits, no problem."

"Okay then," said Martha without further ado. "See you in a week."

The Occupy Wall Street Movement, or OWS as the media often referred to it, had been initiated by an ad in an anti-consumerist Canadian magazine called *Adbusters*. Few could have guessed the way in which it resonated with a populace frustrated with social and economic inequality, corporate control over government decision-making, and the lingering effects of the Great Recession. Though begun in the heart of Wall Street's financial district, eventually Occupy protests spread to more than six hundred American cities and many other countries. Melissa liked the way protestors made decisions through general assemblies, the focus on direct action, and the way in which OWS seemed to energize larger institutional groups like labor and teachers' unions. Though Melissa had long supported LGBT rights, she had a soft spot in her heart for all social justice movements. The 1960s had civil rights and Vietnam protests, the 1980s had struggled against apartheid and US intervention in Central America, and now it seemed like their moment had come, complete with its own anthem: We Are the 99%! Melissa didn't want to miss it.

On a chilly afternoon four days later, Ruth came to Martha's office with news from Melissa. Ruth and Melissa had a particularly close relationship, abetted by the fact that Ruth often referred to her as "mija," which she explained was an affectionate way of saying "my daughter."

"I got the rundown from Melissa last night," Ruth began. "She said they came to power spray the plaza outside of City Hall last night at 2 AM. And that the police are purposely bringing homeless people with mental health issues and dropping them off at the encampment."

Martha shook her head in disgust. Just then, Julia came in to the office and stood next to Ruth.

"What's going on?" she asked.

"I'm just telling Martha some of the things Melissa says are going on at Occupy River City," answered Ruth.

"I read that yesterday they protested about foreclosures at a Wells Fargo bank," Julia quickly added.

"That must have made Melissa happy!" said Martha with a chuckle.

"Yes, she mentioned that," said Ruth. "But she also said they are running really low on food and wanted to know if we could bring some sandwiches or something. I told her I would check with the gang and see what we could do."

"We could meet at my house after work," offered Julia. "I'd like to get my boys in on it too."

"Bueno pues," said Ruth. "I'll pick up some sandwich meat and bread. You in?" she asked Martha.

"I'd like to, but I've got a lot of grading to do tonight. But tell you what," she added. "Why don't the two of you get an early start on it? I'll hold down the fort here." She handed Ruth some money, which she begrudgingly accepted.

Within weeks, as Melissa predicted, the River City Occupy encampment at city hall had been broken up, abetted by an early winter freeze at the end of November. But the Occupy Movement, despite its short physical presence, had exposed fundamental injustices in American society, and its spirit emboldened other movements for justice among immigrants, fast-food workers, Wisconsin state workers, and the Chicago Teachers Union. It also demonstrated the power of nonviolent resistance and social networking as means of protest and progressive change and stimulated counterhegemonic action on the part of artists, musicians, and filmmakers.

Spring 2012

On a cloudless day with a deep blue sky Martha, Ruth, and Melissa took the morning off from Helping Hands to attend a community forum on health care. Martha's early hopes that the ACA would provide health care access to the low-income clients she had served for years at Helping Hands had been dashed when the governor had adamantly refused to support Medicaid expansion. The forum had been organized by a local progressive congresswoman and heavily publicized by the Council on Community Services of which Helping Hands was a part. It had originally been scheduled to take place at the United Way headquarters, but the response had been so great the venue was moved to a large auditorium on the River City U campus.

"I can't wait to hear what the governor has to say for himself," said Melissa as they settled into their seats. Her contempt for the governor was palpable.

"I'm surprised he even agreed to be a part of this," replied Martha. "He's been heckled a few times at press conferences, and it's clear he doesn't take that kind of criticism very well."

The forum was advertised as a way for all sides to share their comments and concerns about the impending legislation, but it was clear that the state's decision not to accept Medicaid expansion or establish a marketplace exchange would be a hot topic. As speakers assembled behind a long table on the platform the crowd grew quiet, but the respectful hush evaporated when the moderator from the university explained that the governor was regretfully unable to attend and had instead shared a short video. The "boos" started immediately. It was clear this was not going to be an ordinary community meeting.

"What a chicken-shit!" Melissa said as she sat back in her chair and folded her arms across her chest.

The governor's video began to play on the screen above the platform, and the crowd reluctantly quieted. After a few minutes of the governor's voice extolling the natural beauty and independent spirit of the state, the scene changed to the governor seated informally on his desk at the capitol. He wasted no time in stating that he opposed Obamacare because he believed that states should fundamentally be in charge of health care reform.

"Then why haven't you proposed anything you dumb-ass!" a voice shouted from the back of the auditorium. This brought a chorus of boos and claps of support from the assembled crowd. Melissa gave Ruth an enthusiastic high-five. The raucous crowd settled down just in time to hear the governor say "expanding Medicaid would be a fool's errand of adding half a million state residents to a broken system, and I will never support what is not in the best interest of this state." The boos and the catcalls that thundered in response was so loud that the governor's final comments were drowned out.

The moderator remonstrated with the crowd to refrain from such indecorous conduct, and the forum continued. The first person to speak was the CEO of the River City Association of Business. Martha leaned over to Ruth and whispered, "I don't know what he's going to say, do you?" Ruth gave her an "I don't know either" look as the speaker began to introduce himself.

"Taxes have always been an important issue to the business community, but if this state doesn't accept the subsidies that come with Obamacare, we will effectively be sending our taxes to the federal government, and with that money the feds will pay health care premiums for people living in other states. That makes no sense. Paying out taxes and getting nothing in return is bad for business and bad for the people of this state. Portable health care insurance will help create more start-up businesses and potentially bring hundreds of thousands of jobs to this state. Though it is by no means perfect, the Association of Business supports Obamacare!"

The crowd enthusiastically clapped as the speaker returned to his seat. Health insurance premiums were a rising cost to business owners, and Martha had always wondered why businesses were not more supportive of health care reform. Ruth leaned over and whispered, "Well, now you know!"

The next speaker was from a conservative think-tank located in the capitol city. After the introduction, he wasted no words. "Government cannot create jobs; it can only take away jobs that the private sector could offer more efficiently. Therefore, the very premise of Obamacare is flawed." There were murmurs from the crowd, but he continued. "Conservatives want health care reform, but nothing in the Affordable Care Act speaks to our values. We value personal responsibility; we believe there should be penalties for misusing emergency rooms for health care, and work requirements should be included. None of these components are part of Obamacare, and that is why conservatives will continue to oppose this legislation." There was some applause while the speaker sat down but the boos returned as well.

The next speaker was from the Hospital Association. "By law," she began, "hospitals cannot turn sick patients away. This leads to billions of dollars of uncompensated care. Since hospitals can't simply eat these costs, they are shifted from those who can't pay to those who can." Glancing at the business association CEO, she continued. "Extra taxes are levied on businesses and property owners, and other costs are shifted to insured patients. This increases insurance premiums and results in additional charges for everyone. The Affordable Care Act will provide health insurance to hundreds of thousands of people via Medicaid and make insurance more affordable to hundreds of thousands more in our state via the marketplace exchanges that will be set up." She swiveled and directed her gaze at the representative from the think-tank. "This will help contain costs and reduce the burden on emergency rooms. This is why the Hospital Association supports Obamacare!"

The pro-reform crowd reacted with thunderous applause. The moderator next introduced a representative from the state department of insurance. "The Affordable Care Act provided funding to help states train 'health care navigators.' These navigators will help to educate people who are interested in seeking health care coverage. The state Department of Insurance is in the process of establishing rules and training expectations that navigators must meet. This training is needed to help safeguard the sensitive information that consumers will have to share with navigators and to make sure that navigators do not improperly influence the health care decisions of consumers."

The speaker ended abruptly to a smattering of applause, but it was clear that the crowd was uncertain about the topic. The speaker from the Hospital Association raised her hand and asked the moderator if she could respond to the comments from the Department of Insurance representative. The moderator consented.

"It is true that the Affordable Care Act provides millions of dollars to allow organizations in the state to train navigators. But the previous speaker neglected to include a few very important details. First, the federal government already requires twenty hours of online training for navigators. What the state is proposing is an *additional forty hours* of state-sponsored training, and a $500 registration fee for navigators to take the additional training." In response to this information a smattering of boos could be heard from across the auditorium. "Speaking for myself and not the Hospital Association, I believe that the main purpose of the onerous additional training is to interfere with the ability of navigators to help individuals in this state to access health care benefits." A chorus of boos now descended on the platform and only grew louder when the representative from the Department of Insurance declined to respond.

Melissa leaned over to Martha and Ruth. "How low can this state get?" she asked. "First we refuse to accept Medicaid expansion and federal subsidies, then we refuse to establish a marketplace exchange, and now it's imposing rules to interfere with navigators who are trying to educate the public at no state expense? It's despicable!" It was clear the majority of the crowd felt like Melissa. Martha and Ruth could offer no rebuttal.

On June 28, the Supreme Court answered Melissa's question. In its *National Federation of Independent Business vs. Sebelius* ruling, the court found that while the ACA could not force consumers to purchase health care, it could tax them if they did not purchase it. It also ruled that the federal government could not withhold existing payments and thus coerce states to expand the Medicaid program per new ACA requirements. In effect, states could opt out of the planned Medicaid expansion without suffering financial penalties, but individuals could not. Though it would face future challenges, Obamacare was one step closer to reality.

On a mild September day, Martha spent the morning going over budget figures with the part-time accountant at Helping Hands. The experience heading the investigation into financial malfeasance that took place at The Children's Corner and the feedback she had received from the staff at Helping

Hands induced Martha to adopt stronger budget safeguards and a more open administrative stance on budget issues. Though a necessary part of the nonprofit's operation, Martha had long since made peace with the fact that it would never be her favorite part of the job. Making her way to the kitchen to retrieve her lunch, Martha found several staff members watching a home video of Republican presidential nominee Mitt Romney speaking to what was apparently a gathering of wealthy donors claiming that "47% of Americans pay no taxes." The program continued to replay the video, which had been leaked to *Mother Jones*, a liberal magazine, from an event that had taken place in May.

"Is that true?" Julia asked. "Do half of Americans really pay no taxes?"

Martha's blood began to boil. Predictably, the news was focused on the veracity of his claim, without giving thought to the substance behind it. If half of Americans pay no income taxes, she thought to herself, it is because they are too darn poor to pay income taxes or receive tax credits because they are working poor with children.

"I don't know if it's true or not," replied Melissa, "but if it is it's an indictment of the economy, not poor people."

It was clear Julia wasn't totally satisfied with this answer.

It galled Martha to think that Romney, a son of privilege whose father was a former governor and presidential aspirant, a man whose net worth was over $300 million, could portray himself as coming from humble beginnings and refer to poor people as *entitled*! Her anger rising, she wanted to respond to Julia and tell her that most people paid more in payroll taxes than they did in federal income tax and that poor people pay much more of their income in state and local taxes than the wealthy, but when she opened her mouth all that came out was . . . anger.

After she finished her verbal fusillade against Romney, the room was quiet. Julia was astonished and clearly uncomfortable. Martha uttered a quick apology, grabbed her lunch, and went back to her office.

But Melissa just smiled. In all her years at Helping Hands, she had never once seen Martha lose her cool. Now Martha seemed, well, just a little more human.

Discussion Questions

1. The Affordable Care Act is a landmark piece of legislation that has helped millions of Americans improve their access to health care. Yet despite its successes, the ACA still has many critics from both sides of the political aisle. Though conservative opposition to the ACA has garnered much attention, what critiques have been leveled against the ACA from the liberal perspective? Do you agree with these points of view? Why or why not?

2. Since the passage of the Adoption and Safe Families Act in 1997 states have been required to move toward termination of parental rights if a child has been in foster care for twelve of the prior fifteen months. Given what is known about addiction and cases like Nola's, what tensions exist between the law and the treatment needs of parents with substance use disorders?

3. At this writing, the Occupy Wall Street movement is five years old. What perceptions do you have of OWS and how it was organized? How did it differ from previous movements? Do you view it as a success or a failure, or some mix of both? Explain your reasoning.

4. Do you live in a state that expanded Medicaid or a state that chose not to accept expansion funding under the ACA? What do you think are the primary benefits to the states that chose to expand it? What populations have benefitted the most from Medicaid expansion, or suffered the most from a state choosing not to expand it? Do you think states should have been given funding to reform Medicaid in their own way? Why or why not?

Suggested Readings

Belkin, D., & Korn, M. (2015, February 16). Colleges' use of adjuncts comes under pressure. *Wall Street Journal*. Retrieved from http://www.wsj.com/articles/colleges-use-of-adjunct-instructors-comes-under-pressure-1424118108

Cost, J. (2014, April 21). The conservative case against Obamacare: A restatement. *The Weekly Standard*. Retrieved from http://www.weeklystandard.com/the-conservative-case-against-obamacare-a-restatement/article/787111

Cilliza, C. (2013, March 4). Why Mitt Romney's "47 percent" comment was so bad. *The Washington Post*. Retrieved from https://www.washingtonpost.com/news/the-fix/wp/2013/03/04/why-mitt-romneys-47-percent-comment-was-so-bad/

DePillis, L. (2014, January 11). A watchdog grows up: The inside story of the Consumer Financial Protection Bureau. *The Washington Post*. Retrieved from https://www.washingtonpost.com/news/wonk/wp/2014/01/11/a-watchdog-grows-up-the-inside-story-of-the-consumer-financial-protection-bureau/

Emanuel, E. (2015). *Reinventing American health care: How the Affordable Care Act will improve our terribly complex, blatantly unjust, outrageously expensive, grossly inefficient, error prone system*. Washington, DC: PublicAffairs.

Gitlin, T. (2012). *Occupy nation: The roots, the spirit, and the promise of Occupy Wall Street*. It Books.

Holland, Jesse. (2007). *Black men built the capitol: Discovering African-American history in and around Washington, D.C.* Guilford, CT: Globe Pequot.

Kaiser Family Foundation. (2012, July). A guide to the Supreme Court's Affordable Care Act decision. Retrieved from https://kaiserfamilyfoundation.files.wordpress.com/2013/01/8332.pdf

Kemp, S., Almgren, G., & Gilchrist, L. (2001). Serving the "whole child": Prevention practice and the U.S. children's bureau. *Smith College Studies in Social Work, 71*(3).

Peirce, H., Broughal, J., & Verret, J. (2013). *Dodd-Frank: What it does and why it's flawed*. Fairfax, VA: Mercatus Center at George Mason University.

Price, C., & Eibner, C. (2013). For states that opt out of Medicaid expansion: 3.6 million fewer insured and $8.4 billion less in federal payments. *Health Affairs, 32*(6), 1030–1036.

Rawal, P. (2016). *The Affordable Care Act: Examining the facts* (Contemporary Debates). Santa Barbara, CA: ABC-CLIO.

Sweet, M., & Applebaum, M. (2004). Is home visiting an effective strategy? A meta-analytic review of home visiting programs for families with young children. *Child Development, 75*(3).

Vestal, C. (2015, July 8). On Medicaid expansion, a question of math and politics. Pew Charitable Trusts: Stateline. Retrieved from http://www.pewtrusts.org/en/research-and-analysis/blogs/stateline/2015/07/08/on-medicaid-expansion-a-question-of-math-and-politics

Zwick, E. (Dir.). (1989). *Glory.* TriStar Pictures.

7

The Path Forward

DECEMBER 2012 MARTHA and Dr. Barr decided to meet for lunch to celebrate the re-election of Barack Obama and Dr. Barr's promotion to associate professor at River City University. Martha first met Dr. Barr when, as an assistant professor, she was chosen by the state welfare agency to evaluate the welfare reform grant that Helping Hands had operated with several other community partners. After the welfare reform grant had been cut, Martha and Annabelle, as she preferred to be addressed, had become more than just professional acquaintances. Martha periodically called on Annabelle to help structure evaluation methods for the various programs offered at the agency, and Annabelle found Martha to be a wealth of information on non-profit administration and practice with children and families. She also called on Martha to consult on occasion as she prepared evaluation reports. Martha knew the information that was helpful to her peers in social services, and she provided Annabelle with the front-line perspective from which faculty were often removed. It also helped that they saw each other frequently around the social work building now that Martha was a regular adjunct instructor.

"Congratulations, Annabelle!" Martha exclaimed as they greeted one another at the door to a favorite diner in town. Pop's Place had been in the city for years and continually run by one family. Pictures of the occasional famous person who graced the restaurant hung on the walls around the diner. It was an institution in River City.

As Annabelle reached out to hug Martha, she replied, "Well, you helped me earn tenure, Martha!" Annabelle had created a publishing niche for herself in the area of program evaluation, becoming a go-to person after her work evaluating the welfare-to-work programs that Helping Hands and other programs had implemented around the state. She parlayed her work with state and federal grants into conference presentations and articles in a variety of journals related to social services and policy. Her goal now was to write a book about her experiences in program evaluation and policy change in an effort to share what she had learned with a broader audience.

As they worked on their "meat-and-three" plates, Annabelle described her plans for the manuscript. "Martha, I think the book will be a much-needed addition to academic literature and for the social work classroom. We need to demonstrate that research of this kind not only assists our communities but also provides a wealth of data and real-life examples that politicians and administrators can use in making decisions about program funding. I want to illustrate what we've learned over the years in a readable format and would like to market the book to social work programs around the country."

"That sounds great, Annabelle!" Martha replied enthusiastically. "No rest for you after tenure, eh?"

"Well, it's not just me I'm talking about, Martha," Annabelle replied with a mischievous grin. "I'd like you to join me as a co-author."

Martha was surprised by Annabelle's proposal. While Martha knew a great deal about the world of family policy and social services, it never occurred to her that she might author a book. "I don't know what to say, Annabelle," she replied. "I'm certainly interested in the topic, but I never imagined I'd be an author. Unless I decided to write a book about parenting twins. Now that would be a story!" she laughed.

"I know it's a new idea, Martha, but I've thought about this and it makes a lot of sense," Annabelle offered. "You're really well-qualified to do this. I want to write about the important things that non-profits need to know in applying for and implementing grant-funded projects, and who better than you to join me? And you know we work well together! I really hope you'll consider it."

Martha promised to think about it, and, truth be told, she was excited about the idea.

After a few minutes of small talk, the subject changed to the recent election. "After all that President Obama has been through, from the financial crisis to the passage of health care reform, his victory is a real validation for what he has tried to accomplish," Martha said.

"I can't pretend to understand the American voter," Annabelle replied. "I mean, in 2010 the Republicans gained sixty-three seats in the House and six in the Senate, and then two years later the country resoundingly votes for a president whose every move is going to be countered by the Republicans they just voted in? It doesn't make any sense to me."

"Funny," Martha replied, "I was just talking to Dr. Gault about this very subject. He said that Democrats won a majority of votes in 2010 in many states that went Republican but that they tend to be clumped in districts where they win by a wide margin and then are spread thin elsewhere."

"Because of redistricting?" asked Annabelle.

"Yep," replied Martha matter-of-factly.

"Well, now it makes sense," said Annabelle. "One of my friends from grad school just sent a Facebook post that said Republicans won twice the number of state legislative seats in four states that voted for Obama. At first I just chocked it up to crazy voters but now it seems like that was a manufactured outcome. That's really depressing."

"Well," Martha replied, "students may not think elections are interesting but it's really important. I've always discussed the impact of felon disenfranchisement but now I'm going to include a special section on voting and elections in all my future policy courses."

"Speaking of which," said Annabelle, "I hear good things about your courses from the students."

"Thanks," said Martha while taking a bite of peach cobbler. "I really like working with the students but Allen complains that I'm always grading papers. Luckily, Jessie moved back in after she graduated last summer so the two of them can keep each other busy when I have to hunker down and grade."

"That's right—Jessie graduated! Congratulations!" Annabelle exclaimed. "Another social worker in the house! And how is Brandon doing?"

"He still has another year," said Martha. "And the both of them are talking about grad school. That's where all that adjunct pay is going to go," she added with a chuckle.

"The demands on parents never end, do they?" asked Annabelle.

"Well, if paying for grad school is the toughest thing I have to deal with as a parent then I consider myself lucky," Martha quickly replied. "You know my friend Carlene, right?"

"Yes, we've met a couple of times at Helping Hands," Annabelle replied.

Shaking her head, Martha continued. "Her son came back from Iraq a different person."

"Was he injured?" Annabelle asked.

"He sustained some minor injuries, but he most certainly has PTSD, and maybe concussive head trauma. He's moody and depressed, and he and his wife have split, which has been really tough on Carlene because his wife and baby lived with her while he was deployed."

"I'm so sorry to hear that," said Annabelle.

"To make matters worse, a few of the soldiers in his unit have committed suicide," Martha added. "Carlene is worried sick about him."

"You've probably heard that the school is planning a conference on military social work. It certainly sounds like social work needs to be involved in this issue."

"Yes, I have," said Martha, "but I'm really conflicted about it. Since Carlene's son came home so wounded emotionally, I found myself absorbed in reading about the effects of war on soldiers and their families."

"I would think that would make you enthusiastic about the conference." Annabelle replied.

"Well, as I tell my students, social work has a history of working towards peace, which led to two social workers winning the Nobel Peace Prize," Martha intoned. "Jane Addams and just last year, Leymah Gbowee."

"I'm embarrassed to say that I have never heard of . . . how do you pronounce her name again?" Annabelle asked.

"Leymah Gbowee," Martha repeated slowly. "They made a really powerful film about her a few years ago called *Pray the Devil Back to Hell*. She and the woman who eventually became the president were given the Nobel for their efforts to end the civil war in Liberia."

"She sounds like an amazing woman!" Annabelle exclaimed.

"She definitely is," Martha said. "And Jane Addams was president of the Woman's Peace Party during World War I. Their stories make me think that social work should focus on peace and nonviolence rather than just services to returning vets."

"I get your point about the difference in focus," Annabelle replied. "But it's not like the profession needs to choose between one or the other. That sounds a bit like a false dichotomy."

"Maybe you're right," Martha conceded, "but are there any sessions on peace and non-violence at the conference? Any sessions on how vets, who have seen firsthand what our foreign policy looks like on the ground in places like Kabul and Fallujah, can get involved in organizing for a different set of nonviolent foreign policies?"

Annabelle was silent for a moment. "I see what you're saying, Martha." She leaned back in her seat and refolded her napkin. "It goes back to an old tension in social work, right? Should it focus on cases or causes?"

"That's interesting," Martha replied. "I hadn't heard it put like that before."

"So let me shoot from the hip here," Annabelle continued. "There's been a push to integrate these sorts of problems and policies across the curriculum. Do you have any suggestions for how I could include these topics in the research methods and data analysis courses I teach?"

"That's a good question!" Martha put her fork down and thought about it for a moment. "I know there was a report that came out not too long ago from a Johns Hopkins researcher that estimated the total number of civilian casualties in Iraq to be over 600,00. And there's a website called Iraq Body Count that estimates over 100,000 civilians have been killed."

"That's a lot of variation," Annabelle interjected.

"Yes, it is," replied Martha. "So perhaps you could have students investigate the strengths and weaknesses of the different methods these studies use, or even if there are any surveys that capture how Americans feel about civilian deaths in Iraq and Afghanistan. And of course, there has been a great deal of attention given to suicide rates among returning U.S. soldiers . . ."

Annabelle was already lost in thought, thinking about the different ways she could integrate the subject into the research methods course she was set to teach in the coming semester.

Martha continued. "This semester in my social justice course I asked students to imagine the following: what could we accomplish if we spent $4 trillion on social welfare programs like we have spent in Iraq and Afghanistan?"

"We've spent *four trillion dollars*?" asked Annabelle, back from her momentary reverie.

"Over twenty years or so, that's the estimate," Martha replied. "The students crunched the numbers and came up with some amazing alternatives."

"Give me an example," Annabelle asked quickly.

"To be honest, the students had trouble finding reasonable ways to spend all the money," Martha replied while mentally conjuring some of the proposals.

"Ah, c'mon, give me something!" Annabelle chided. "You've got the numbers side of my brain all fired up!"

"Okay, here's one that comes to mind," Martha said as she took out a pen and began to write on a napkin. "The nurse who came to train us in the Family Partnership Model said that in England every newborn receives something called a *maternity grant*. My students took that idea and ran with it. So, every year in the United States about four million children are born. If we gave each family with a newborn a thousand dollars, how much would that be?" she asked.

"Well, that's easy," Annabelle replied. "A thousand times a million is a billion, so that would be four billion dollars."

"Right," said Martha. "Now, no doubt a thousand dollars to help pay for a newborn would help a lot of families, but one of my student groups proposed that every family receive a grant of $20,000. How much would that be?"

"Okay, now you're getting up there. Basically that would be twenty times four billion, or eighty billion."

"You're a whiz, Annabelle," Martha joked. "So how much would we spend if we ran the program for ten years?"

"Eight-hundred billion," came the quick reply.

How about twenty years?" Martha kept pushing.

Annabelle was up to the challenge. "That would be $1.6 trillion."

"And that's the point the students made," Martha continued. "We could give every child born over the next generation a $20,000 birth allowance and it still wouldn't add to half of what we will spend in Iraq and Afghanistan."

"That's amazing, Martha! I imagine that would pretty much wipe out poverty for those young families as well."

"It would," said Martha. "Of course there are always implications to such big social innovations, but the idea of a guaranteed income in one form or another is gaining steam around the world."

"I don't think a policy like that would ever gain a foothold here," replied Annabelle. "There's just too much emphasis on individual responsibility and a 'pull-yourself-up' bootstraps mentality."

"Yeah?" Martha replied in a way that let Annabelle know that a surprise was coming. "What if I told you that a guaranteed income program already exists in the United States?"

"Is this a trick question?" asked Annabelle with a grin.

"Nope," replied Martha. "Totally on the up and up." Annabelle stared at Martha, waiting for the answer. "Have you ever heard of the Alaska Permanent Fund?" asked Martha.

"No, I haven't," Annabelle replied.

"Well, the permanent fund provides every state resident of Alaska a guaranteed income."

"Really?" Annabelle replied with incredulity.

"Absolutely," said Martha. "It's funded mostly on taxes levied on the petroleum industry. In fact, in 2008 when Sarah Palin was talking up rugged Alaskan values every four-person household in that state received over $8,000 in income from the fund."

Annabelle stared at Martha with a stunned look on her face. "I'm trying to figure out why I've never heard of that before!"

"And I'll bet you've never heard that Richard Nixon proposed a guaranteed income in the early '70s either," Martha added.

"Now you're just piling it on!" Annabelle exclaimed with a smile. She was clearly impressed with just how much Martha had done as an adjunct professor to become so well-versed in subjects outside of her area of practice. She complimented Martha on her commitment. "I don't know how you do it all Martha, but I wish I could get students so involved in a class."

"Well the last thing I want to do is be caught looking like I'm not prepared. The students will check Google during class to see if you've got your facts straight!" Martha said with a laugh.

When the plates had been cleared, they began to discuss the evaluation report of the home visiting program that Helping Hands had recently received.

Annabelle took a folder of papers from her briefcase. "I looked it over last night, and I think there are some really interesting findings that Helping Hands might use to expand the services."

Martha was all ears. Helping Hands was about to apply for a round of funding and wanted to add support services that did not exist in River City. In what could only be construed as a stroke of fortuitous luck, the home visiting program that Helping Hands began a few years earlier had presaged the Maternal, Infant, and Early Childhood Home Visiting program that was included as part of the Affordable Care Act (ACA). The Maternal Infant, & Early Childhood Home Visiting program, or MIECHV, as it was called, provided $1.5 billion in grant funding to states and localities to promote home visiting programs in distressed communities. This represented a thousand-fold increase in federal support for this type of service. Martha's twist on traditional home visiting programs added social workers and interprofessional education to a formula that typically consisted of nurses and pediatricians. As a result, in addition to the focus on maternal and newborn health, the program run by Helping Hands also focused on improving family economic stability via coordinated case management and community referrals. Because the program had been successful at reducing risk in families, Helping Hands now intended to apply for MIECHV funding to continue the program after the original funding had ended.

"As you know, the findings show that you're most effective when working with two-parent families," Dr. Barr said. "Single parents in the program were helped too, but they didn't show the same progress that two-parent families did. That's not surprising really, as the couples could support one another while single parents weren't able to bundle resources in the same way."

Martha was shaking her head.

"What?" asked Annabelle.

"I still can't believe what we stumbled into," replied Martha. "When we put the grant together I had no idea that MIECHV funding would be coming down the pike. And unbelievably, several of our outcomes, like reduced ER visits and increases in family economic stability, are part of the six outcome domains emphasized by MIECHV."

"I get what you're saying," Annabelle interjected, "but I don't think it's as coincidental as you make it out to be. I mean, you researched the issue and saw a need in the community that was going unmet. And to me, it makes sense that a home visiting program would be part of the agenda for health care reform, which had been brewing for years."

"So, just a 'great minds think alike' kind of thing, huh?" added Martha jokingly.

"Exactly!" agreed Annabelle with a big smile. "And speaking of economic stability, the social workers on the team were identified as particularly helpful in finding crucial support. Just about every qualifying household received WIC and SNAP, which significantly reduced rates of food insecurity. And many of the families received Earned Income Tax Credits for the first time because they received free tax consulting as part of program participation."

"You know," Martha cut in, "I'm often the first one to criticize the lack of benefits we provide to struggling families, but I'd like to think I'm fair enough to recognize when as a society we do something right. Social programs may be lacking, but they can still help needy families. WIC eligibility is automatic if the household qualifies for SNAP or Medicaid, so it was just a matter of training the team members to recognize the families who were eligible for multiple services. And ARRA increased the Earned Income Tax return for families so it was a no-brainer to make sure all eligible families applied for and received that benefit."

Annabelle nodded her head in agreement. Martha's grasp of policy in a rubber-meets-the-road kind of way was impressive. But it was clear that the social workers in the program didn't just sign their clients up for benefits. They also created support services that were lacking and that brought tangible benefits to program participants. In the qualitative comments section in the evaluation report the low-income participants raved about the support groups that the social workers had put together, which helped bring parents together with others facing similar issues and problem-solve as a group. As the report made clear, the social work component was an integral part of the home visiting program.

Martha smiled. She was certainly proud of what Hayley and Melissa had accomplished. But she was also impressed with the ways in which the nursing team helped the young parents to better care for their children. It was clear that the staff learned from practicing together and that the interprofessional model of practice advanced the mission of the program.

As they continued to talk, they both agreed that two major groups were in need of help but often neglected. Young fathers who had separated from the mother or were otherwise not living full time with their children were often ignored. The nurses and social workers commented that social services often did not view young fathers on an equal footing with the mothers. Martha was well aware of the more pernicious stereotypes of young, low-income fathers, but in her experience only a small fraction of them were indifferent to their children. Most of the young men the visiting program worked with wanted a meaningful relationship with their children but often succumbed to the stress, the streets, or negative turns in their relationship to the mother of their child. Using a strengths-based perspective, Martha believed that visiting programs could do a better job of supporting parental caregiving among young fathers. She had researched "fatherhood" programs and knew that strong programs made a difference. Her staff had been successful at engaging some of the young men, but they also encountered barriers to including them in the parenting of their children.

The other group for which Martha felt particular compassion since the Family Partnership program began was single mothers with addiction histories. She remembered Nola, who had "fallen off the wagon" while trying to care for her premature infant, and her husband DJ, without whom she surely would have lost custody of their baby boy. Without the intensive services and support of the team at Helping Hands, the entire family might have fallen apart. The last time she had seen Nola and DJ was on a trip to the supermarket, where the couple was also shopping with their young son. Martha made it a rule to not approach clients in public places, but Nola had come across the produce department to thank Helping Hands for their faith in her and the staff's willingness to advocate for her. According to Nola, the program did more than help her recover from addiction; it saved her marriage and put their family on stable ground for the future. Martha knew that Nola's success was clearly tied to her husband and his support as she completed treatment and learned to use all her resources to maintain sobriety. Single mothers simply need more supports from the community.

Dr. Barr shared that both ideas had merit and recent research indicated that each group could see positive outcomes when programs were targeted to their specific needs.

"You know, Martha," she replied, "you could get federal funding from different agencies within Health and Human Services to do what you're suggesting. Evidence-based models recommended by the Substance Abuse and Mental Health Services Administration can be found on their website. Residential-based programs that act essentially as supportive housing for parenting and sobriety exist and have proven successful. Some have been around since the early 1990s, so there is considerable research on those models."

She continued, "I also read an article recently about a program that targeted young fathers and worked to teach them how to care for their children from infancy on. Its primary belief is that young fathers are left out too often, and, unless there is a serious reason not to, they can and should be more involved with their children. In fact, from a methodological standpoint a consensus is forming about what constitutes an effective fatherhood program."

"Do tell," said Martha with enthusiasm.

"Well," began Annabelle, "as with most research, the gold standard is to have a treatment and control group. "Sample sizes should be large enough in both groups to draw significant conclusions; I'd say about thirty minimum. Programs should maintain a majority of the original sample all the way to the end. Finally, there should be an independent evaluation and evidence of a significant positive change in one or more outcomes."

"That's quite a list coming right off the top of your head!" Martha exclaimed.

"Well, I do teach the stuff," Annabelle said modestly in reply.

Martha smiled. When she first met Annabelle she couldn't believe how young she looked. But that first impression had quickly given way to a more seasoned accounting of Annabelle's intellect, dedication, and competence. In that instant Martha knew that she wanted to pursue the book project with Annabelle, but she also knew that adding another project to her busy schedule would no doubt cause more stress in her personal life. Putting aside that thought, Martha returned to the topic at hand. "That's a straightforward list, but even so, those would be challenging goals for a community non-profit to meet."

"In what ways?" asked Annabelle.

"Well, it seems like it would take an intensive effort to recruit that many participants and a low client-to-staff ratio to keep participants engaged and prevent dropout. Those considerations would probably scare off most community programs from the get-go."

"That's what often happens," replied Annabelle. "Everybody touts 'local solutions to local problems,' but when it gets down to actually doing the work, few community organizations have the resources or the wherewithal to implement empirically viable programs."

"Sounds like that should be a chapter in your book," Martha responded with a smile.

"You mean *our* book!" Annabelle quickly shot back. It was a nice gesture, and Martha was amazed at how quickly the idea of co-authoring a book had taken root.

Returning to work after her lunch meeting, Martha was filled with anticipation. She was intent on adding important components to the next round of the home visiting program and excited about the prospect of helping Annabelle write a book. She paused, however, when she thought about Allen's likely reaction. Martha knew that Allen's expectations about what their lives would look like after the twins went to college had gone unmet. With the agency cutbacks and the increased need brought about by the lingering recession, Martha had been busier than usual. Allen's job was steady, with little fluctuation, but hers seemed like a rollercoaster tied to the economy and the multiple dramas playing out in the lives of Helping Hands clients and staff.

It didn't help that she now spent her nights grading papers and preparing for classes. Martha knew that something would have to give, and she didn't want it to be her marriage.

Summer 2014

Martha was ready to present the first evaluation report on the new MIECHV program to the board of directors. Helping Hands had applied for and received MIECHV funding the previous year. The new iteration of the program had added a robust mentoring program for young fathers. Reverend Anderson, one of the partners in the welfare-to-work grant from a few years earlier, had been running an informal mentoring program for young men through his church. He had eagerly accepted Martha's invitation to be a partner in the home visiting grant and adapt his program to focus on young fathers. The grant included funding for a recruitment coordinator and modest stipends for mentors and young fathers who participated in the program. Despite these enhancements, the evaluation report noted that the program was having a trouble recruiting a sufficient number of mentors. Many balked at the significant training that was required or could not commit to the time demands and face-to-face meetings that were part of the program's expectations. Martha hoped that the board would allow her to ease the training requirements, and perhaps increase the stipend amounts available to mentors. Otherwise, the program was off to a good start, abetted by the fact that it had been a continuation of the home visiting program that Helping Hands had started a few years earlier.

Julia popped her head in Martha's door. "I just sent PDF copies of the evaluation to the board members. Do you need anything else?"

"No," said Martha. "I think that should do it."

Down the hall they could hear Hayley and John arguing about President Obama's recent decision to send US troops back to Iraq to counter a growing insurgency from the Islamic State of Iraq and the Levant, commonly referred to as ISIL. Hayley, the self-described "Mennonite feminist," was decrying the reintroduction of US armed forces in to the region while John, the former Army medic, argued the need for the United States to finish the job it had started in 2003.

"They're at it again," said Julia, shaking her head.

"I'm not sure they ever really stop," Martha replied. It was a curious relationship, but somehow the two of them made it work. Martha had asked each of them privately if they wanted to work on a separate nurse-social worker team and had been surprised when neither of them wanted to make a change.

As far as Martha could tell, they had learned to balance their contrasting styles and put the needs of clients first, but it sure made for some interesting lunch hour debates.

"What's on your schedule for the rest of the day?" asked Julia.

"I'm going to meet with Associate Dean Morris at River City U," replied Martha.

"What about?" asked Julia quickly in her typical nosy fashion.

"I don't know," said Martha. "I assume it's about course scheduling, but she was very clear that she wanted to meet in person."

Later that afternoon, Martha knocked on the associate dean's door.

"Come in, come in, Martha!" came the reply.

The associate dean was responsible for hiring adjunct instructors and scheduling all the courses. Martha had always found her to be personable and extremely well organized. The School of Social Work at River City U, like most large schools, used a significant number of adjunct instructors, and the courses often had to be scheduled far in advance. It was a significant undertaking.

Martha was offered a seat at a circular mahogany table. "Thank you for coming in, Martha. How are you?" Dean Morris asked.

"I'm fine, thank you," Martha answered with a smile. It was clear the meeting was going to be about more than course scheduling.

"How is your book with Dr. Barr coming along?" she asked.

"Well, we submitted a draft, and now we're just waiting to hear from the reviewers," Martha answered.

"That can be a nerve-wracking part of the process," Dean Morris replied.

"Well, it's all new to me," said Martha, "but I've really enjoyed working with Annabelle, and we're hoping for the best."

"I'm sure it will all work out," said Dean Morris reassuringly. "And I want to let you know that it is quite impressive for you to co-author a book while being an executive director of an agency *and* teaching as an adjunct instructor! Where do you get the time to do all these things?"

"Quite frankly," Martha answered, "lately it doesn't seem like I have had the time to do anything well."

"Well," said Dean Morris as she took out an envelope filled with student course evaluations, "your spring teaching evaluations belie that statement. They are very strong, Martha! Clearly you thrive in the classroom."

"Oh, well, thank you," said Martha, a bit squeamish about receiving such praise from the associate dean. "I think it helped that it was a particularly interesting time to be teaching a course about social policy."

"In what ways?" asked Dean Morris.

"Well, we spent a great deal of time discussing the ACA, and the botched rollout on Healthcare.gov."

"What a fiasco!" interjected Dean Morris. "Here we have the biggest piece of health care legislation in fifty years and with three years to prepare the government can't even get a website to run smoothly? It spoon fed to the public the conservative notion that government is too inefficient to organize any large undertaking."

"It didn't help that half of Congress seemed to be rooting for it to fail while voting repeatedly to repeal Obamacare," Martha quipped in response.

"True enough," came the reply, "but surely that can't explain the subpar performance of the website. What do you think was behind it?"

"As we discussed in class," Martha replied, "it seemed to be a confluence of things. Big start-up jobs like this always encounter problems. The federal contracting system is out of date and cumbersome, and the job was given to incumbent vendors rather than cutting-edge companies with a track record of success. Another big issue is that no one seemed to have predicted the huge demand that would immediately be placed on the system. I mean, millions of people tried to sign up on the very first day!"

Dean Morris was obviously enjoying the spirited back and forth. "I've never taught a social policy course," she said, "but I can imagine that it makes the course more interesting when policies are rolling out in real time."

"It certainly does," Martha said while nodding her head In agreement. "We also had the opportunity to discuss the fallout from the Supreme Court decision to invalidate key provisions of the Voting Rights Act, and the various restrictions on abortion access that several states have passed. I'd like to think that there was never a dull moment."

"Judging by your scores and the comments, Martha, I'd say the students would agree!" said Dean Morris with obvious satisfaction. She put the student evaluations back in the envelope and slid them across the table to Martha. "Which brings me to my next point. Martha, I've asked you here today because I'd like to offer you a clinical faculty position here at the school."

Martha sat for a minute in stunned silence.

Dean Morris continued with details of the offer. "It would be a ten-month appointment. We would like you to teach a range of classes, provide supervision for students doing fieldwork, and participate on various committee assignments. I'm adding a tenth month of salary because I would like you to be the faculty liaison for all adjunct faculty. It's a new position, and I think you would get us off to a great start."

"I don't know what to say," Martha finally replied. "I thought we were going to be discussing my teaching schedule!"

"Well," responded Dean Morris in a jovial manner, "in a way we are! I see it like this, Martha, with your teaching record and forthcoming publication, you already have your foot halfway in the academic door. I'm just formally inviting you to step in full-time. Regarding salary, though I doubt we can match what you are making as an executive director, we'll do our best to make it competitive. And of course, you can always earn additional income by teaching a course or two in the summer."

Dean Morris spent the next fifteen minutes answering questions about the position and then walked with Martha outside to the front of the building.

She shook Martha's hand and told her how excited she would be to have Martha join the faculty at the River City School of Social Work.

The next day, as was her custom, Martha was up early. She and Allen had discussed the offer the previous evening. Somewhat surprisingly, he had been neutral about the decision. He pointed out the pros and cons of remaining at Helping Hands versus taking the offer from River City U but otherwise wanted the decision to be hers. Martha had been at Helping Hands for so long she had never really contemplated a career change, but she was confident that Melissa, Ruth, and Julia could provide steady leadership and maintain the Home Visiting Program and other services that Helping Hands offered if she were to leave.

As she walked down the driveway to pick up the morning paper, she looked down the street to the Johnson's house. Sadly, Mr. Johnson had passed away the previous year, but the dahlias blooming off the front porch let Martha know that Mrs. Johnson was doing okay. Martha remembered how exhilarating it had been when the neighborhood came together to defend the Johnson's home. Her partner in that endeavor and former Helping Hands board member Florence Bossier was now working with the NAACP to investigate the "robo-signing" foreclosures that had been perpetrated by large mortgage companies. Apparently, loan companies had foreclosed on thousands of homeowners without even being able to legally prove that they owned the properties in question. It was a reminder that important aspects of the housing crisis, the crisis that had sent the American and international economies into free-fall, were still unresolved.

Martha glanced at the headlines and saw that another unarmed, African American male had been shot and killed by the police. This had happened on other occasions in River City over the last six months. The story followed a familiar line: initial obfuscation by official police sources, followed by the media's focus on the criminal history of the victim. The extra-legal killing of young Black men had been the focus of a report Martha had required as reading in her policy class the previous semester. Martha remembered the Rodney King beating by the LAPD in 1991 and the deadly riots that ensued when all the officers were acquitted. Looking over the article Martha wondered if another such riot was on the horizon. The article noted that a candlelight vigil and protest was being held at Rev. Anderson's church. It was an event that Martha planned to attend. "Enough is enough" she thought to herself as she walked back to the house.

WILL MARTHA DECIDE TO LEAVE HELPING HANDS?

As she sat in the kitchen reading the paper in the morning quiet, she suddenly knew what she wanted her future to look like. "Allen," she said getting up and walking down the hall, "I've made my decision."

Discussion Questions

1. In the lunch meeting between Martha and Dr. Barr, in regards to the intersection between the military and social work Annabelle brings up a

historical tension between "cases" and "causes." What do you think this means? What are some examples of this tension from social work history? Can you think of contemporary examples? Discuss.

2. The ACA was fully implemented in 2014—though many states have refused to expand the Medicaid program and receive generous federal subsidies. What has been your experience with the ACA as a consumer and as part of any professional experience within social work? If you had the chance to choose between the ACA and a Medicare for All system as recently proposed by Democratic presidential candidate Bernie Sanders, which would you choose?

3. A number of well-known films have been made about the Great Recession and the rampant speculation that led to an international financial melt-down. These include *Capitalism: A Love Story* (2009), *Inside Job* and *Company Men* (2010), *Too Big To Fail* and *Heist: Who Stole the American Dream?* (2011), *The Queen of Versailles* and *Arbitrage* (2012), *The Big Short, 99 Homes,* and *Plunder: The Crime of our Times* (2015). Despite these films and the outrage they expressed toward the corporations seen as responsible for the Great Recession, the Obama administration made an explicit decision *not* to criminally prosecute any corporate executives (though stiff fines without an admission of guilt were often handed out by federal agencies). What are the pros and cons of the Obama administration's decision?

4. The end of the chapter presages the shooting of eighteen-year-old Michael Brown in Ferguson, Missouri, on August 9, 2014, and the beginning of the Black Lives Matter (BLM) movement. What are the protest tactics and explicit policy goals of the BLM movement? How are these similar to and different from previous civil rights efforts?

Suggested Readings

Alaska Permanent Fund Corporation. (n.d.). Retrieved from http://www.apfc.org/home/Content/publications/reportArchive.cfm

Bleiberg, J., & West, D. (2015, April 9). A look back at technical issues with Healthcare.gov. Brookings Institute. Retrieved from https://www.brookings.edu/blog/techtank/2015/04/09/a-look-back-at-technical-issues-with-healthcare-gov/

Daley, D. (2016). *Ratf**ked: The true story behind the secret plan to steal America's democracy.* New York: Liveright.

Dayen, D. (2016). *Chain of title: How three ordinary Americans uncovered Wall Street's great foreclosure fraud.* New York: New Press.

Disney, A. E., & Reticker, G. (2008). *Pray the devil back to hell*. Roco Films Educational.

Dursa, E. K., Reinhard, M. J., Barth, S. K., & Schneiderman, A. I. (2014). Prevalence of a positive screen for PTSD among OEF/OIF and OEF/OIF-era veterans in a large population-based cohort. *Journal of Traumatic Stress, 27*, 542–549.

Edin, K., & Nelson, T. (2013). *Doing the best I can: Fatherhood in the inner city*. Berkeley: University of California Press.

Halperin, M., & Heilemann, J. (2014). *Double down: Game change 2012*. New York: Penguin Books.

Johns Hopkins School of Public Health. (2006, October 11). Updated Iraq survey affirms earlier mortality estimates. October 11. Retrieved from http://www.jhsph.edu/news/news-releases/2006/burnham-iraq-2006.html.

Manza, J., & Uggen, C. (2008). *Locked out: Felon disenfranchisement and American democracy*. New York: Oxford University Press.

Maternal, Infant And Early Childhood Home Visiting Programs (MIECHV). (n.d.). National Conference of State Legislatures. Retrieved from http://www.ncsl.org/research/health/maternal-infant-and-early-childhood-home-visiting.aspx

Returning home from Iraq and Afghanistan: Preliminary assessment of readjustment needs of veterans, service members, and their families. (2010). Washington, DC: National Academy Press.

Schott, L. (1985). The Woman's Peace Party and the moral basis for women's pacifism. *Frontiers: A Journal of Women Studies, 8*(2), 18–24.

Sure Start Maternity Grant. (n.d.). Retrieved from https://www.gov.uk/sure-start-maternity-grant/overview

Afterword

THIS BOOK IS a sequel to *Caught in the Storm: Navigating Policy and Practice in the Welfare Reform Era* (Lyceum Books, 2010). In that book, we created Martha White, an insightful and hard-working executive director of a small community-based non-profit in the fictional metropolis of River City. Martha was (and is!) a composite of the many talented people we worked with for years as we evaluated community-based welfare-to-work and substance use prevention programs in Texas. Martha and the staff at Helping Hands, the agency she directs, are excellent examples of the people in every community, many of whom are trained social workers, who provide nongovernmental social services to low-income and vulnerable populations. We set *Caught in the Storm* in the aftermath of welfare reform legislation passed in 1996 by President Clinton and amid the devastation wrought by Hurricane Katrina in August 2005. Little did we know that as we submitted the book to the publisher, the United States (and indeed the world) economy was beginning the worst economic tailspin in seventy years: the aptly named Great Recession. Thus, as soon as *Caught in the Storm* was finished it was clear that a sequel, rather than a new edition, would be in order.

The Great Recession taught many lessons. One that came at an enormous cost is that the US financial system was built to discriminate against average homeowners and workers to benefit groups of wildly avaricious but politically well-connected speculators. This context gave rise to the presidential campaign of Barack Obama, then just a junior Senator from Illinois. With soaring oratory, an emphasis on hope, and clear-headed analysis, Senator Obama tapped into the millennial generation as a political force and won the 2008 election in an electoral landslide. However, once in office, the newly elected president faced double-digit rates of unemployment, millions of homes in foreclosure, and an economy in freefall. We decided it would be good to tell the story of how the Great Recession looked from the ground up and to show how agencies like Helping Hands struggled to adapt to the deteriorating conditions and intense need that enveloped almost every American community.

Despite the attention that policy and structural reform received during the Great Recession, and the importance the social work profession places on social justice, we continued to meet with students who questioned their own ability to make a difference in the policy realm. As one undergraduate told us, she had no real memory of the world before the Iraq War and the War on Terror. From this vantage, militarism and inequality can seem to be the norm, as accepted as smartphones and bailouts for the very financial institutions that brought the world economy to the brink of collapse.

But we must work for change. The millennial generation, through no fault of their own, has been handed a bill of goods. They were raised in a post 9-11 world, and many will reach adulthood and raise their own families in a post-industrial world of economic and environmental volatility, ballooning personal debt, endless war, and the increasing privatization of the public sphere. The news in their lives demonstrates a form of state-sponsored terror over the daily experience of African Americans, a denial of climate science with potentially devastating effects, and an election of a president who lost the popular vote and stands diametrically opposed to many if not most of the values that social work holds dear. That is why we felt it important to highlight Melissa's participation in the Occupy movement and Martha's organized effort to oppose the foreclosure and eviction of her elderly neighbors.

For students who see themselves as mental health professionals, child welfare workers, gerontological practitioners, anti-poverty activists, or one of many other possible positions in the field, we hope this book will spark an interest and strengthen a belief in your ability to influence policy. Like Martha and the staff at Helping Hands, you have the passion and training to make a difference in your community. Since its (their) earliest days, social workers have used effective policy practice to improve the lives of vulnerable populations and strengthen communities. Social workers simply cannot leave the policy work to others; otherwise we risk ending up with policies that ignore, punish, and ultimately do great damage to those we serve. Being a true social worker means engaging in policy practice. It is that distinction—a focus on advocacy, policy analysis, policy development, and social change—that makes social work unique among the helping professions.

We hope you enjoyed reading this book and find in it the spark to share your talent, inspiration, and professional skills with others. Based on our recent experience, we are encouraged that a new generation of passionate social workers stands ready to tackle the challenges that lie ahead.

Spanish Terms

Bienvenidos!: Welcome

Quisás: Perhaps

Que pasó, pues?: What happened?

Basta ya!: Enough already!

Fíjate: Can you believe it?

Que pasa, pues?: What's happening?

Mejor tarde que nunca: Better late than never

Dios mío: My heavens

Bueno pues: OK then . . .

Index